Why Cope

When You Can

Conquer?

Studies in Selected Psalms

JUANITA PURCELL

REGULAR BAPTIST PRESS
1300 North Meacham Road
Schaumburg, Illinois 60173-4806

Quotations on pages 8 and 85 are from *Falling into Greatness* by Lloyd John Ogilvie. © 1984; Thomas Nelson Publishers, Nashville. Used by permission.

Quotations on pages 38 and 48 are from *When Heaven Is Silent* by Ronald Dunn. © 1994; Thomas Nelson Publishers, Nashville. Used by permission.

Quotations on pages 61, 63, 70, 78, 90, 91, and 93 are from *Exploring the Psalms,* 2 vols., by John Phillips. © 1986; Loizeaux, Neptune, NJ. Used by permission.

Quotation on page 84 is from *The Power of Encouragement* by Jeanne Doering. © 1982. Used by permission.

Quotation on page 99 is from *Mount Up with Wings* by Joyce Hart. © 1998. Used by permission.

CONTENTS

DEDICATION

TO MY FAVORITE PREACHER, J. O.

Even though you have retired as a pastor from a local church, I know you will never retire from preaching. You will always be my pastor and favorite preacher. I still have the privilege of hearing you speak each week, and you always challenge and bless my heart. We've been serving the Lord together for over thirty-four years, and it just keeps getting better and better. Thank you for all the spiritual enrichment you have added to my life.

PREFACE

A few years ago I spent three years studying the Psalms. Each day I pondered the truths, plodded through the tough verses, and prayed many of the psalmists' prayers. My time in the Psalms always reminded me of God's power and providence in my life. I was also challenged time after time that *God is good* even when He doesn't seem good. I wrote the book *Be Still, My Child* as a result of those daily times in God's presence. As you can imagine, the book of Psalms became very precious to me.

When I decided to write a Bible study on the Psalms, I had a hard time deciding which of the 150 psalms to use in the study. All the psalms have such interesting lessons to teach us. I decided to focus on some of the psalms that could move us from just coping with life to conquering.

Worry and discouragement are two common problems we all struggle with. They are attitudes that keep us from conquering. But a daily dose of Psalms can help. A. C. Gabelein said, "A psalm a day keeps worry away." Athanasius said, "Most Scripture speaks to us, while the Psalms speak for us." When we are down and discouraged and need to be lifted up again, we can find help in Psalms. Often we can identify with the psalmist and say, "That's just how I feel."

No other book confronts the real-life perplexities and problems we face today like Psalms. And no other book can move us from coping to conquering like the Psalms.

How to Live a Happy Life

Psalm 1

"And he shall be like a tree planted by the rivers of water, that bringeth forth his fruit in his season; his leaf also shall not wither; and whatsoever he doeth shall prosper"
(Psalm 1:3).

Psalm 1 almost serves as a preface to the rest of God's hymnbook, the book of Psalms. We don't know who wrote this psalm, but the message is clear and simple: the righteous are blessed, the wicked are cursed.

The first word in Psalm 1 is "Blessed." The Hebrew word for "blessed" often means "happy"; however, this word has a much broader meaning than the one we usually use for "happy." We most often think of happiness as a feeling we experience when circumstances and people are favorable. The word "blessed" relates to the internal calm a believer enjoys when things are right between her and God. This calmness produces contentment and joy in her life.

This psalm is full of truth that many of us have lived out and experienced. Loving God, I am happy; living in God, I am safe; obeying God, I will experience His rest. God wants to bless us; He wants us to enjoy the blessed life He has planned for us; but we must meet His conditions for receiving blessings. We will look at those requirements in this lesson; then you can evaluate how you measure up. My prayer is that you will discover the key that opens the door to true happiness if you have not already found it.

The Blessed Man (vv. 1–3)
Read Psalm 1:1–3.

1. Why are so many Christians unhappy?

2. How would you describe ungodly counsel? See Proverbs 14:12.

3. Notice the progression of the three words in verse 1: walketh, standeth, sitteth. When a Christian turns to the ungodly for counsel, what else might he do with the ungodly?

> "Ungodly people are all around us. . . . The ungodly can live in our homes, work with us, be among our best friends. Taking their advice is fatal. The blessed person does not slow down to walk with them. If he does, his walk will soon come to an immobilizing standstill."[1]

4. What do you think the psalmist meant by the "law of the LORD" (v. 2)? See Psalm 119:9–11.

5. Happiness is not found in the world. Happiness is found in the Word, the "law of the LORD." What comes to your mind when you read, "his delight is in the law of the LORD"?

6. How can you find delight in reading the Bible?

7. Do you go through the "motions of devotions"? To find out, ask yourself this question several hours after you have read your Bible: What did I get from the Word today?

"The quiet time often becomes a hollow convention of religious structure, instead of a holy meeting with the personal Christ. We read a verse or two of Bible, pray a little prayer and—oops! It's 7:30, Amen, and off to work again. . . . Some of us have forgotten why we take time, and with Whom we spend it. Instead of thinking of devotions in terms of what we want from God, perhaps some of us need to re-evaluate. . . . Have you devoted yourself to looking for Him with all your heart and all your soul?"[2]

---

8. The happy, fulfilled child of God is described by four graphic phrases in verse 3. What are they, and what do they mean to you?

9. The happy Christian is pictured as a strong tree planted by rivers of water. (a) What is the significance of the words "rivers of water"? Read John 7:37–39.

(b) Why is the tree a picture of strength?

10. As strong trees, we are to be productive—not just stand around looking good, as some trees do. What kind of

fruit should be evident in a Christian's life? Read
Galatians 5:22 and 23.

---

*"What a garden of virtues. In these nine quali-
ties—the fruit of the Spirit—we have one of the
most concise and complete biographies of God.
For these are His qualities, His attributes. This is
what God is like. And God's greatest desire for us
is to become like Him. As we live in Him and He
in us, it is natural for us to be blessed, bear fruit
and prosper, as the First Psalm declares."[3]*

---

11. What is the significance of the words "bringeth forth his
fruit in his season"?

12. Happy Christians are not green just in the spring. They
are like evergreens; they just keep growing: "Their leaf
also shall not wither." How would you describe a Christian who does not wither? Read Jeremiah 17:7 and 8 and
Habakkuk 3:17–19.

13. Do you have a hero of the faith or a spiritual role model
who demonstrates this kind of perseverance? If so, write
down what that person endured.

*"Herein we as Christians are to differ from the
world. When hell is let loose, and the worst comes
to the worst, we are to do more than 'put up with
it' or 'be steady.' We are to know a holy joy and
manifest a spirit of rejoicing. We are to be 'more
than conquerors,' instead of merely exercising
self-control with the aid of an iron will. We are to
rejoice in the Lord and to joy in the God of our
salvation."4*

14. What kind of prosperity does the happy Christian enjoy?
    Read 1 Corinthians 1:4 and 5 and 2 Peter 1:3–8.

*". . . God is promising prosperity of life rather than
of bank accounts. He is assuring those who obey
Him and honor Him that in their obedience and
trust they will find enrichment of life. This will
mean far more to their true happiness than any
amount of material prosperity."5*

The Ungodly Man (vv. 4–6)
Read Psalm 1:4–6.

Grain consists of kernels, straw, and chaff. Chaff, which
covers the kernel, has no value at all, while the kernel and
straw do. In Bible times, after the head of the grain was
pounded to separate the kernel from the chaff, the grain was
tossed into the air. The wind blew the chaff away, and the
grain fell back to the threshing floor.

15. A tree is a picture of strength and stability. What does
    chaff picture?

16. Why would the ungodly be compared to chaff? Read John 14:27 and Isaiah 48:22.

17. The unbeliever "shall not stand in the judgment" (v. 5). The ungodly won't have a leg to stand on when they are told their names are not in the Book of Life. What arguments for gaining Heaven might they use?

18. This psalm describes two ways to live and two ways to die. What are the two ends and to whom are they assigned?

19. How does the radical difference between the righteous and the ungodly motivate you to delight in God's Word?

"The ungodly man is condemned to perish, however we have the assurance that God cares for His own (v. 6a). Our Heavenly Father may need to discipline us at times, but He always takes special care to preserve us in the midst of every situation. The unbeliever, however, has no hope of preservation. His doom is certain. Not only does he face the problems of this present life but also the prospect of God's wrath and the second death (Rev. 21:8; cf. 1 Cor. 6:9,10; Gal. 5:19–21)."[6]

---

20. Which of these descriptions fits your life: the blessed, happy person or the ungodly, hopeless person?

After studying this lesson, maybe you realize for the first time that you do not have eternal life. Or maybe you realize you have been depending on your good works to get you to Heaven. If you are not absolutely sure you have eternal life, read the verses that follow. They are the difference between Heaven and Hell.

• God **loves** you and wants you to enjoy the **abundant life** He offers you—John 3:16; John 10:10.

• Man is **sinful,** and his sin **separates** him from God—Romans 3:23; Romans 6:23.

• Jesus Christ's death is the only **provision** God has made to pay for man's sin—Romans 5:8; John 14:6.

• You cannot earn Heaven by your good works—Ephesians 2:8, 9.

• You must **receive** Jesus Christ as your Savior before you can personally experience His love for you and the abundant, happy life He has planned for you—John 1:12.

• You can invite Christ into your life right now by a simple act of **faith**—Romans 10:9–13.

Are you ready to invite Christ into your life to be your Savior? Use the following prayer to help you express your desire to God: "Lord Jesus, thank You for dying on the cross for my sins. Right now I open my heart and invite You into my life as my Savior. Thank You for forgiving my sin and giving me everlasting life. I want You to control my life so I can experience the blessed life You have planned for me."

• The Bible **promises eternal life** to all who receive Christ as Savior—1 John 5:11–13.

 From My Heart

If you really want to live life with a capital L, I recommend the "Vine life." "Vine life" is living out the commands of John 15:1–5, where Jesus says He is the vine and we are the branches. If you disconnect a branch from the vine, what happens? It withers up and dies. Only as the branch is connected to the vine can the sap keep flowing into the branches. Only as we stay connected to the Vine (Christ) will His life flow through us so we can continue to grow. We stay connected to the Vine by spending time in His presence each day and reading and meditating on His Word. When we learn to live the Vine life, our "leaf also shall not wither; and whatsoever [we do] shall prosper."

From Your Heart

Have you found the key that opens the door to happiness? Do you draw your strength for daily life from Christ? Do you display determination and consistency in your life? Do you feel rich because of your inward prosperity? Are you living the Vine life?

Notes:

1. Lloyd John Ogilvie, *Falling into Greatness* (Nashville: Thomas Nelson Publishers, 1984), p. 18.

2. Patrick M. Morley, *I Surrender* (Brentwood, TN: Wolgemuth & Hyatt, Publishers, Inc., 1990), pp. 167, 168.

3. Leroy Brownlow, *The Fruit of the Spirit* (Fort Worth: Brownlow Publishing Company, Inc., 1982, 1989), p. 7.

4. D. Martyn Lloyd-Jones, *Faith Tried and Triumphant* (Leicester, England: Inter-Varsity Press, 1987), p. 60.

5. Stuart Briscoe, *What Works When Life Doesn't* (Colorado Springs: Chariot Victor Publishing, 1976), p. 20.

6. John White, *Songs That Touch the Heart* (Schaumburg, IL: Regular Baptist Press, 1994), p. 11.

Listen! God Is Speaking

Psalm 19

"Let the words of my mouth, and the meditation of my heart, be acceptable in thy sight, O LORD, my strength, and my redeemer" (Psalm 19:14).

Psalm 19 presents God's wordless communication to us through His creation and His verbal communication through His Word, the Bible. David, the writer of Psalm 19, spent many years as a shepherd and then as a fugitive running from Saul before he became a king. This shepherd had seen many mornings bursting with the nonverbal affirmation of God's majesty and glory. Consequently, Psalm 19:1–6 reflects the words of one acquainted with observing the heavens.

Without using a word, God communicates His might and deity to us each day in the things we see. However, this wordless communication is limited; that is why we need the written Word. The message from Psalm 19 is clear: we can know about God through wordless revelation, His creation, but we can know Him intimately only as He reveals His heart and mind to us through His written Word, the Bible. Psalm 19:7–14 gives us a picture of how God reveals Himself to us. Only through the Scriptures can we meet and really get to know God personally.

God Speaks in the Heavens (vv. 1–6)
Read Psalm 19:1–6.

1. God reveals Himself to all the world through His creation; He speaks a universal language. Consider the fact that days come and go with total reliability. We know exactly what time the sun will rise and set. What does this predictability tell you about God? See also Hebrews 13:8.

15

2. Nature preaches thousands of sermons to the heart of man. (a) Each day there is l_____ and d_____. (b) Each year there is s_____, s_____, f_____, and w_____. (c) Every person experiences l_____ and d_____.

> " 'There is a God' all nature cries,
> I see it painted on the skies,
> I see it in the flowering spring,
> I hear it when the birdlings sing,
> I see it in the clouds that soar,
> I hear it when the thunders roar,
> I see it when the morning shines,
> I see it when the day declines,
> I see it in the mountain's height,
> I see it in the smallest mite,
> I see it everywhere abroad,
> I feel, I know there is a God."[1]

3. Psalm 19:4 says God "set a tabernacle for the sun." The sun is the most dominant feature in our sky. What would happen if the sun stopped shining?

4. David compared the sun to a bridegroom coming out of his chamber and a strong man running a race. What do these illustrations mean to you?

5. Have you ever vacationed near a lake or ocean? If so, what will you see people doing each morning and evening? Why do they do this?

"The sun is 93 million miles from the earth. Is it a coincidence that it is precisely the right distance away to permit life on earth? What if it were closer? We would burn up. What if it were farther away? We would freeze to death. Is it a coincidence that the moon is 240,000 miles from the earth? What if it were closer? The gravitational pull would be so strong there would be enormous tidal waves. Truly the heavens are telling us about our magnificent and awesome God. He is absolutely dependable in keeping the universe in perfect order. The meteorologists can tell us exactly what minute the sun will rise and set each day. God is always on schedule—never too early and never too late."[2]

As wonderful as God's creation is, it is not enough. The picture of God is too vast, remote, and vague. Mankind needed more revelation, so God gave us written revelation. The first six verses of this chapter focused our attention on the nonverbal communication of God to man through His creation. Our attention is now turned to the verbal communication of God to man through His written revelation, the Scriptures.

God Speaks in the Scriptures (vv. 7–11)
Read Psalm 19:7–11.

6. Can you imagine what it would be like to have never heard the Word of God? Have you ever led someone to Christ who had never heard the Word of God before? Explain the experience.

7. The Scripture is referred to in many different ways in these verses. List the various names for the Word of God in verses 7–11.

8. We may read books that are helpful and enlightening, but they are not perfect like the Word of God because they are written by imperfect people. (a) What can the law (teachings) of the Lord do that men's words cannot do?

(b) What portion of the Word of God did you hear that convinced you of your need to be saved?

9. "The testimony of the LORD is sure"—it does not change. It is a solid foundation upon which to build our lives. Even the most unwise people who build their lives on it can become wise. Why?

10. The statutes (orders) of the Lord are the pathway to happiness. (a) Why is this road not heavily traveled even though it guarantees a blessed, happy life? Review Psalm 1.

(b) God's orders for our lives are always right. How have these orders brought rejoicing to your heart lately?

---

*"The Scriptures provide us direction without equiv-
ocation. But this in itself poses a problem because
most human beings are a bundle of contradic-*

> *tions. They want an authoritative statement just so long as it tells them with authority that it is OK to do what they intend to do! . . . God does not work that way. He spells things out, explains what to do, what not to do, and how to do it or not do it as the case may be. He then promises what will happen and leaves the choice to the individual. Whether you feel inclined to obey or disinclined to obey, you can be equally sure of what will happen. God has spoken."*[3]

11. The commands of the Lord are pure, or clear. How do they enlighten us? Read Psalm 119:11 and 105.

12. What does "the fear of the LORD" mean? Should we be afraid of God?

13. How does the fear of the Lord affect our lives?

14. God's judgments are always true, or trustworthy, and right, or just. How does this differ from human judgments?

> "Pray do not find fault with man that limps—
> Or stumbles along the road, unless you have worn
>   the shoes he wears—
> Or struggled beneath his load.

There may be tacks in his shoes that hurt, though
    hidden from view,
Or the burdens he bears placed on your back—
Might cause you to stumble, too.

"Don't sneer at the man who is down today—
Unless you have felt the blow that caused his fall,
Or felt the pain that only the fallen know.
You may be strong, but still the blows that were his,
If dealt to you in the selfsame way at the selfsame
    time—
Might cause you to stagger, too."[4]

15. Have you found God's Word more precious and satisfying to you than material possessions and gourmet food? Explain how this can be.

16. Why do some Christians not heed God's warning in His Word (v. 11)?

"Does it impress you that we have more time-saving devices than ever before in this computer world, yet we seem to have less time?. . . (Believe it or not, I have the whole Bible at my fingertips and can call up any verse or verses in the Bible in about 2 seconds.) But we are still in a hurry! We seem to have less time for spiritual things. We are so busy. It is not wrong to be busy; you are to be commended for your diligence. But it is wrong if you are too busy for the Lord. Do you have a daily quiet time with the Lord? When you take time to pray, read the Bible, and wait on the Lord—giving Him His rightful place—hours are never lost. They are gained."[5]

17. Psalm 119 describes the results of obeying God's Word. Skim through that psalm and list some of those results.

18. Review Psalm 19:7–11. What does the Word of God do?

Verse 7

Verse 8

Verse 9

Verse 10

Verse 11

Why don't you take a moment right now to thank God for all the men and women who have faithfully taught you God's Word over the years and have encouraged your spiritual growth. As you mention them before the Lord, ask the Lord to encourage them wherever they are right now. You may even want to write a note of thanks to one or more of the people for whom you are thanking God.

God Speaks to the Soul (vv. 12–14)
Read Psalm 19:12–14.

19. Reading and heeding God's Word leads to this heart-
    searching question: Lord, what are my secret faults?
    Take a moment to examine your heart. Ask God to
    convict you of any hidden sins in your heart. If God
    convicts you of something, don't say, "Lord, forgive my
    sin." Instead, say, "Lord, forgive my sin of (name the
    sin)."

20. The Old Testament provided for sins of ignorance, or
    innocence, but not presumptuous sins (Leviticus 4; 5).
    (a) List some things you would consider presumptuous
        sins.

    (b) How could the prayer in verse 14 keep us from
        presumptuous sin?

21. Many Christians are more concerned about being
    acceptable, or right, in their peers' sight than in God's
    sight. Where do you fit?

 From My Heart

    Would you like to be a stronger Christian? Would you
like to have more faith, more peace, more contentment?
These things are yours for the taking when you learn to read
and heed God's Word each day.

Emerson said that if the stars came out only once a year, everybody would stay up all night to watch them. We have seen the stars so often we hardly even notice them anymore. We have taken this blessing for granted. Have you been taking the Word of God for granted? Has it become "old hat" to you?

If you want to put some life into your devotional time, I suggest that you keep a journal each day. Here's a way to do it. Read the Bible verses suggested in the devotional book you are using. Then read several verses before and after those verses to understand the verses in their context. Select one verse that is especially meaningful to you. Read the thoughts in the devotional book. Now you are ready to write in your journal. Write down your selected verse, and write a prayer to the Lord, telling Him how you want to use that verse in your life that day. You will find that keeping a journal gets you out of the devotions rut and makes God's Word come alive.

From Your Heart

Are you reading the Word of God each day? Are you heeding what you are reading? If you are not reading the Word daily, will you start today?

Notes:

1. Robert Parsons, *Psalms of Victory* (Chicago: Moody Bible Institute, 1966), p. 24.

2. Juanita Purcell, *Be Still, My Child: 366 Devotional Readings from the Psalms* (Schaumburg, IL: Regular Baptist Press, 1997), p. 51.

3. Briscoe, *What Works When Life Doesn't,* pp. 81, 82.

4. Eleanor Doan, compiler, *The Speaker's Sourcebook* (Grand Rapids: Zondervan Publishing House, 1960), p. 137.

5. Charles U. Wagner, *Winning Words for Daily Living* (Grand Rapids: Kregel Publications, 1989), pp. 85, 86.

Why Fear?
The Shepherd Is Near!

Psalm 23

"The LORD is my shepherd; I shall not want" (Psalm 23:1).

Psalm 23 is the pearl of the Psalms, the most familiar of all the psalms to most readers. Some say it is the sweetest, simplest song that was ever sung. It is also called the "He/me" psalm. Seventeen times the writer, David, refers to himself, and thirteen times to the Lord.

> "The **LORD** is **my shepherd;** **I** shall not want.
> **He** maketh **me** to lie down in green pastures:
> **he** leadeth **me** beside the still waters.
> **He** restoreth **my** soul:
> **he** leadeth **me** in the paths of righteousness for **his**
>   name's sake.
> Yea, though **I** walk through the valley of the shadow
>   of death,
> **I** will fear no evil:
> For **thou** art with **me;**
> **thy** rod and **thy** staff they comfort **me.**
> **Thou** preparest a table before **me** in the presence of
>   **mine** enemies:
> **thou** anointest **my** head with oil;
> **my** cup runneth over.
> Surely goodness and mercy shall follow **me** all the
>   days of **my** life:
> And **I** will dwell in the house of the **LORD** for ever."

Untold numbers of believers have lived by this psalm, and, in the faith of it, multitudes have died.

In this psalm David, who was a shepherd, is not speaking as a shepherd but as a sheep. He speaks with a sense of love and devotion. Perhaps David wrote this psalm in the latter years of his life. The psalm reflects the maturity of many years of experience and a heart mellowed by many trials.

As you study this lesson, my prayer is that you will be reminded afresh of our Lord's greatness. I trust you will also have a settled confidence in your heart that He is everything you will ever need for every situation you will ever face.

Read Psalm 23.

Verse 1

1. To get the full significance of verse 1, we need to know Who the "LORD" is. If you have a Hebrew lexicon or a Bible dictionary, trace the word "LORD" in this verse. What does it mean?

"What a world of meaning, then, lies wrapped up in the word 'LORD' in the first verse of this Psalm! Jehovah who is all-faithful, never failing in His promises, almighty, all-powerful, who is able to supply all of our needs, who created the heavens and the earth, who upholds all things by the word of His power, who spake and it was done, who commanded and it stood fast; . . . the 'LORD' who, speaking to the multitudes, said, 'I am the good shepherd; the good shepherd giveth his life for the sheep'—such a Shepherd, faithful, powerful, sympathetic, is our 'LORD.' What a wealth of meaning, then, lies in the first clause, 'The LORD' (who is LORD, and Lord)—such a 'LORD' is 'my Shepherd.' "[1]

---

2. "The LORD," Jehovah God, is our sovereign caretaker and manager. What do the following verses tell you about the Lord's control?

Isaiah 40:25 and 26

Psalm 147:3–9

Acts 17:24–28

3. How does it make you feel when you realize the Controller and Manager of the universe is also your manager and controller?

4. Read John 10:11. When Jesus became God incarnate among men, what was one of His titles?

5. Every shepherd had a herd of sheep. What do you think the shepherd's main responsibility was?

> *"He said, 'I am the good shepherd.' He, better than any other, knew the sheep He had undertaken to save, and He knew the Shepherd's duties. . . . He knows that [sic] He has to do with very silly sheep, who have no strength to protect themselves, no wisdom to guide themselves, and nothing to recommend them but their utter helplessness and weakness. But none of these things baffle Him. His strength and His skill are sufficient to meet every emergency that can possibly arise."[2]*

6. If you have access to an encyclopedia, see what you can find out about sheep; then answer the questions in the left column on page 27. Using your Bible, answer the corresponding question in the right column.

How the Shepherd Cared for His Sheep

a. Why did the shepherd cut a mark on one of the sheep's ears?

b. Why would the shepherd not let the sheep eat in rotten soil but only in healthy pastures?

c. Why did the shepherd constantly watch his sheep?

d. Why did the shepherd have to protect the sheep from wild animals?

e. When sheep were too feeble or weak to walk, the shepherd carried them. Why?

How Our Good Shepherd Cares for Us

a. We are graven on the Lord's hands (Isaiah 49:15, 16). How does this describe His care for us?

b. What kind of food does our Shepherd provide and why? Read Matthew 4:4.

c. Our Shepherd knows our nature to stray. Read Psalm 139:7–10 and describe His care for us.

d. We need the Shepherd's constant protection from the enemy. Why can we feel safe in enemy territory (Psalm 18:2)?

e. The Shepherd knows we will be weak at times. What will He do for us when we feel we can't keep going (Isaiah 46:4)?

Verse 2

Sheep are like people: they can't lie down and rest when they are full of fear. Sheep are dependent on the shepherd to take them to green pastures where they can rest. We can have the sense of grazing in green pastures, free from fear, when we know the Shepherd is with us and is guiding us.

7. When we are full of fear, our first response is to run from the circumstance that is disturbing us. When we remember Who our Shepherd is, what can we do (Psalm 4:8)?

> "Fear not, little flock, He goeth ahead,
> Your Shepherd selecteth the path you must tread;
> The waters of Marah He'll sweeten for thee,
> He drank all the bitter in Gethsemane.
>
> Fear not, little flock, whatever your lot,
> He enters all rooms, 'the doors being shut;'
> He never forsakes; He never is gone,
> So count on His presence in darkness and dawn."[3]

The shepherd takes the sheep to water because he knows they need it. Our Shepherd, the Lord Jesus, knows we need the living water, His Word. He provides circumstances to encourage us to drink from the well that never runs dry.

8. What is the significance of "still waters"? Read Psalm 46:10.

Verse 3

In Psalm 42:11 David describes himself as "cast down." A "cast down" sheep is one who is on his back and can't get up by himself. Have you ever hit bottom and felt you couldn't get back up? David was there at times. However, he knew the One Who could restore his soul and his joy. This same God wants to restore our soul when we are cast down.

9. Sins like worry, bitterness, and anger burden us down and rob us of joy. (a) How do we get our joy restored? Read Psalm 51.

(b) What burdens do you need to leave at Jesus' feet so He can restore your soul?

"David recalls how tenderly God had dealt with him after his backslidings and how graciously and completely He had restored him to fellowship. . . . Poor wandering soul, have you fallen by the wayside? Have you become a wayward sheep? Have you wandered from the fold? Are you tossed about, wounded, sick and sore? Do you desire to come back again to the Shepherd's care? Come now, right now, while the throb of passion is still beating high, while the deed of shame is recent; while the blot of sin is still wet."[4]

The shepherd always led the sheep into good pastures so they could get the proper food and water they needed in order to stay healthy. If they looked sickly and scraggly, his reputation as a shepherd was at stake. The Lord wants to lead us in the paths that He knows will be good for us.

10. Why is it so important that God's children, the sheep of His pasture, walk right before others?

11. The Lord wants to lead us, but He gives us the choice of filling our bellies with poison weeds or good grass. What if we fail to follow? Will He chasten us with His rod and staff? Read Psalm 119:67 and 71.

Verse 4

Somewhere between Jerusalem and the Dead Sea was a valley called the "Valley of Death." It was a narrow passageway between two mountains where wolves waited for prey. Without the shepherd leading them, with his rod and staff to protect them, the sheep would be fearful of entering the valley. Notice we *"walk* through the valley of the shadow of death." We would like to *run* through the valley experiences, but God wants us to walk through them. We must remember when we are in the shadows that the shadow is a reflection of the real. Sometimes the shadow of death is worse than the real.

> *"It is a great art to learn to walk through the shadowy places. Do not hurry; there are lessons to be learned in the shadow that can never be learned in the light. You will discover something about His ministries you never knew before. His rod and His staff they will comfort you—the one to guide, the other to protect you, and the sheep that are nearest will know the most of both. When we go into the valley of the shadow of death we come so near Him that we look into His face and say, not 'He is with me'—that is too formal, too far away— but 'Thou art with me.' The need and the usefulness of Christ is seen best in trials."*[5]

12. When we reflect on what we think is going to happen, it can be twice as bad as bearing the actual trouble. Psalm 23:4 says, "I will fear no evil." (a) Why is there no need to fear the valley experiences? (Also see Hebrews 13:5.)

(b) What valley experience have you gone through lately? How did you handle the experience?

"The worst evils of life are those which do not exist except in our imagination. If we had no troubles but real troubles, we should not have a tenth part of our present sorrows. We feel a thousand deaths in fearing one, but the Psalmist was cured of the disease of fearing."[6]

The shepherd would use the rod to beat off the wolves when they attacked the sheep. He used his staff to pull up the sheep when they would fall into ravines and other places where the shepherd's help was needed. What a comfort to know that our Shepherd's rod and staff protect us and correct us.

13. (a) What dangers have come upon you unawares when you sensed God's care and protection in your life?

(b) Why does God correct us when He sees we are going astray (Hebrews 12:6)?

Verse 5

The shepherd would go out early in the morning to prepare the pasture for the sheep. He would make sure there were no poisonous weeds to hurt them or animals to attack them. In the evening when he brought them into the sheepfold, he would put oil on their heads where parasites would hide and irritate their skin. The healing touch of the shepherd made the sheep feel good again.

14. God has provided protection for us against the enemies that would attack us. (a) What enemies can lurk in our minds?

　　(b) How does God help us deal with these enemies? Read Isaiah 26:3 and 4.

15. How should we respond when we think of God's good provisions for us? Read John 15:11.

Verse 6

　　Sometimes the shepherd had sheep dogs that followed the sheep and helped the shepherd keep the sheep from going astray. Someone has said that "goodness and mercy" are the sheep dogs that follow us to help keep us in the right path.

16. Read the following verses and describe some of the ways God showers His goodness on us.

　　Ephesians 4:32

　　Philippians 4:13 and 19

　　Isaiah 26:3

17. Read the following verses and describe how God demonstrates His mercy to us.

    Titus 3:5

    Lamentations 3:22 and 23

    Psalm 138:8

    Someone has said we have to learn only two things in this life: how to live and how to die. David had learned them both! He knew the Lord was everything He would ever need in life and would be everything he would need in death.

18. Have you learned how to live and how to die? Are you positive you will dwell in the house of the Lord forever when you die? How can you be sure that you have eternal life and will never lose it? Read Romans 10:9, 10, and 13.

    Do you believe Christ died, was buried, and rose again to pay for your salvation? Have you confessed with your mouth you believe Christ died for you and asked Him to save you? If so, John 10:25–29 says you have eternal life; there is no end to eternal. To guarantee the security of our salvation Christ gives us a beautiful picture in John 10:28 and 29. We are in Christ's hand, and God's hand is over His; nothing can take us out of their hands. We are secure!

From My Heart

Marvin R. Vincent said, "This peaceful idyll (the twenty-third psalm) is a voice out of the maturer life of the psalmist, out of memories of care and battle and treachery; a voice that tells that peace and rest of heart depend not upon the absence of life's burdens, nor on the presence of nature's tranquilizing scenes, but solely upon the shepherding of God."[7]

This lesson is written with the voice of my "maturer life." As I was writing this lesson, I looked through my old lessons on the Twenty-third Psalm. I had taught four different lessons over the past twenty-five years. The lessons changed as I changed. Years of burdens and trials have tendered my heart and my perspective on life and my great God. Twenty-five years ago I sang the chorus "Christ is all I need, Christ is all I need, All, all I need." I sang the words, but I didn't really believe them in my heart. Today I can sing those words and with full confidence say, "The LORD is my shepherd; *I shall not want.*" Christ is everything I will ever need for every situation I will ever face.

When I say . . .	God says . . .
"It's impossible"	"All things are possible" (Luke 18:27)
"I'm too tired"	"I will give you rest" (Matthew 11:28–30)
"Nobody loves me"	"I love you" (John 3:16)
"I can't go on"	"My grace is sufficient" (2 Corinthians 12:9)
"I can't figure things out"	"I will direct your steps" (Proverbs 3:5, 6)
"I can't do it"	"You can do all things" (Philippians 4:13)
"I'm not able"	"I am able" (2 Corinthians 9:8)
"I can't manage"	"I will supply all your needs" (Philippians 4:19)
"I'm afraid"	"I have not given you a spirit of fear" (2 Timothy 1:7)
"I'm always worried"	"Cast all your cares on Me" (1 Peter 5:7)

"I'm not smart enough"	"I will give you wisdom" (James 1:5)
"I feel all alone"	"I will never leave you" (Hebrews 13:5)

From Your Heart

Do you believe Christ is all you will ever need for every situation you will face? Are you living like you believe that? What problems do you have in your life right now that you need to give to God? What are you going to do with what you have learned in this lesson?

Notes:

1. William Evans, *The Shepherd Psalm and Looking Beyond* (Chicago: Moody Press, 1921), pp. 17, 18.

2. Hannah Whitall Smith, *The God of All Comfort* (Chicago: Moody Press, 1956), pp. 58, 59.

3. Paul Rader, quoted by Mrs. Charles E. Cowman, *Springs in the Valley* (Grand Rapids: Zondervan Publishing House, 1968), pp. 278, 279.

4. Evans, *The Shepherd Psalm,* pp. 35, 37, 38.

5. W. Y. Fullerton, quoted by Mrs. Charles E. Cowman, *Streams in the Desert,* vol. 2 (Grand Rapids: Zondervan Publishing House, 1966), p. 34.

6. Charles H. Spurgeon, *The Treasury of David,* vol. 1 (McLean, VA: MacDonald Publishing Company, n.d.), p. 355.

7. John Comper Gray and George M. Adams, compilers, *Gray and Adams Bible Commentary,* vol. 2 (Grand Rapids: Zondervan Publishing House, n.d.), p. 489.

The Way Back from Failure

Psalms 32; 51

*"Restore unto me the joy of thy salvation;
and uphold me with thy free spirit" (Psalm 51:12).*

Psalms 32 and 51 are David's prayers of repentance. To understand the sin he was confessing and repenting of, you must read 2 Samuel 11 and 12. In these passages you will see David's failure, fall, and faith. Surely these verses walk us through one of the darkest chapters in David's life.

King David was probably about fifty years old at this time in his life. How could such a great man commit such a great sin? He loved God and had fought for God; he had served God for over thirty years. How could he do it? The same way you and I can if we get out of the will of God. Apparently David was not where he should have been—at war with the rest of the soldiers. David failed to follow his path of duty; he took off his armor and decided to rest. When we get out of God's will and take off our spiritual armor (Ephesians 6:11–18), we cannot depend on divine protection.

David may have been in bed all day. Second Samuel 11:2 says he arose at eventide, just after sunset. He saw Bathsheba bathing and sent his servant to bring her to him. Remember, this was not a hot-blooded youth. David was fifty years old. He had many wives and grown sons.

When we let ourselves become consumed with lust, all reasoning of what is right and wrong goes out the window. David was king; his sons watched him; his followers watched him as an example of righteousness. In an unguarded moment, he was surprised, seduced by his thoughts, and led away captive by Satan. He was "drawn away of his own lust, and enticed" (James 1:14).

In Psalms 32 and 51 we will see the awful hurt and pain that accompany sin. God forgives the worst of sins. (David

36

committed adultery and murder.) But the consequences of
sin are still there. The child that Bathsheba bore died
(2 Samuel 12:22, 23); David's son Amnon raped David's
daughter Tamar (2 Samuel 13:1–20); later David's son
Absalom tried to usurp the throne (2 Samuel 15:7–12).

As you study this lesson, my prayer is that you will
realize that you can fall into sin so quickly if you don't walk
close to Christ each day. If a man as great as David could
fall, so can you and I!

Read Psalms 32 and 51.
David's Failure
1. It was springtime, the time to go to battle again
   (2 Samuel 11:1). (a) Assuming David was fifty years old,
   what might have been his excuse for staying home?

   (b) How do we use similar excuses?

2. Does God intend for us to stay home and leave the
   spiritual battles we once fought? Why? Read 2 Timothy
   4:7.

"The older I get, the more tempted I am to say, 'Let
someone else do it; I'm tired; I've done my part.'
However, God will not let me do that. God's
instruction is always to stay in the battle. Don't
quit! You and I, like Paul, must keep pressing
toward the mark (Philippians 3:14). If you've
decided to sit at home and 'let someone else do it,'
. . . remember what happened to David!"[1]

David's Fall

Psalm 32 pictures a man in turmoil over his sin. It is probably a description of David's struggle with the guilt and shame of his sin of adultery with Bathsheba. His misery was intensified when he had Bathsheba's husband murdered to cover his sin.

3. Read Psalm 32:1–5. How do these verses describe David's misery?

"Memory can be a minister one minute and a monster the next. We have memories we run to and memories we run from. . . . But eventually they overtake us. At some unguarded moment, they pounce on us, bringing with them all the disappointments of the past. . . . Memory is the video camera of the mind; it records everything, forgets nothing. You may think it has forgotten, but something, a word, an insignificant incident, a song, a smell—anything can trigger the memory, and suddenly it's dragging barbed-wire through your stomach."[2]

---

4. Psalm 32:3 reads, "When I kept silence." When did David admit his sin before man and God? Read 2 Samuel 12:1–14.

5. (a) Have you ever tried to hide your sin from God? How did you feel?

(b) How could Psalm 139:7–12 be an encouragement to parents with a wayward child of God?

David's Faith

6. In Psalm 32:2 and 5 and Psalm 51:1–3 David confessed his sin, iniquity, transgression, and guile. It seems David wanted to cover every base to describe the depth of his sin. Give your definition of the four words David used in his confession.

Sin

Iniquity

Transgression

Guile

"Do you feel God could never forgive you for what you have done? Have you committed murder? Have you committed adultery? David did! Is your sin greater than David's? I have good news for you: NO SIN IS TOO GREAT FOR GOD TO FOR-GIVE! God will forgive any sin when confession comes from a truly repentant and contrite heart. The only thing God may not do is erase the consequences of that sin. You, like David, may have to live with the results of your sin the rest of your life. However, you can live as a free person.

*You are no longer in bondage to that sin, dragging
it around wherever you go. The New Testament
records nothing of David's sin. He is remembered
by God, not for his moral failure, but as 'a man
after mine [God's] own heart' (Acts 13:22)."[3]*

7. David's first words in Psalm 51 were for mercy. He then
   asked to be washed and cleansed. What do these words
   tell us about how David felt? Read Psalm 51:2, 3, and 7.

8. David was in a sad state of mind and body when he
   finally confessed his sin to God. To add to his sadness
   and grief, he realized what a dishonor his sin was to God
   (2 Samuel 12:13, 14). (a) Did he try to justify his sin or
   shift the blame? What did he do (Psalm 51:4)?

   (b) How do people today shift the blame for their sin?

*"As long as we refuse to take the blame, or blame
others for our own wrongdoing, we'll never know
God's renewal and restoring power. David could
have said, 'It's really not my fault, you know—it's
Bathsheba's.' . . . Or he could have blamed his
father. After all, he was always left out as a kid. Or
then again, he could have accused his brothers
who never accepted him. But he didn't do any of
these things. He owned the sin himself—it was his
alone—and began to talk to God about it."[4]*

9. In Psalm 51:10 and 12 what do the words "renew a right spirit" and "restore unto me the joy" tell us about David?

10. Can you relate to David? Were you ever in a backslidden condition with a bad spirit and no joy? How did God renew your spirit and renew your joy?

> *"O that you may have grace to plead with God, as though you pleaded for your very life—'Lord, renew a right spirit within me.' He who sincerely prays to God to do this, will prove his honesty by using the means through which God works. Be much in prayer; live much upon the Word of God; kill the lusts which have driven your Lord from you; be careful to watch over the future uprisings of sin. The Lord has His own appointed ways; sit by the wayside and you will be ready when He passes by."[5]*

11. In Psalm 51:11 David prayed, "Take not thy holy spirit from me." How was the Holy Spirit's presence in a believer's life different in the Old Testament than in the New Testament? Read 1 Samuel 16:14; John 14:16; Romans 8:9; 1 Corinthians 3:16.

12. A sinning saint does not lose her salvation (John 10:28), but what does she lose? Read Psalm 51:12 and 1 John 1:7–9.

13. Some people say a murderer cannot go to Heaven. They believe God cannot forgive the sin of murder. What sin or sins does God list as unforgivable (1 John 1:9)?

14. The New Testament does not give any record of David's sin. Rather, he is described as "a man after mine [God's] own heart" (Acts 13:22). Why do you think God was so merciful and gracious to David? Read Psalm 51:15–17.

15. Do you know a backslidden Christian who has fallen so many times he/she has given up? How could you use Psalm 51 to encourage that person?

> *"Maybe you're saying, '. . . but you don't know my circumstances. Right now I'm defeated by the problems I'm experiencing. I'm having some hard times.' If you are defeated by your circumstances, let me suggest an antidote for you. Begin reading your Bible to find a specific promise from God, and then start claiming it. Start expecting God to act, and you will find that God's promise will inject new hope into a hopeless situation. Real success often begins at the point of failure."*[6]

16. We are not failures if we fall. We are failures if we won't get up and try again. What might the apostle Peter have remembered about his past that could have caused him to quit? Read Matthew 26:34, 35, and 69–75.

17. David learned some valuable lessons in this dark chapter of his life, and he was ready to teach transgressors what he had learned: "Then will I teach transgressors thy ways; and sinners shall be converted unto thee" (Psalm 51:13). What might David have taught transgressors that would have converted them or turned them back to God? See Hebrews 11:25 and Galatians 6:7 and 8.

18. We've learned some great truths in this lesson that we can teach backslidden believers. However, backsliders usually don't want to hear what we have to say. What must we do to get an entrance into their hearts?

 From My Heart

My heart is so grieved when I counsel with people who have messed up their lives but will not face their sin. They want to shift the blame for their sin to someone else. Often they want to blame their mate; sometimes they shift the blame to their parents; some may place the blame on their jobs. The list could go on.

David did not shift the blame for his sin to Bathsheba. He knew God had seen the vile thoughts in his heart and mind before he brought Bathsheba to his room. It was time to be honest with God. David was full of godly sorrow that led to repentance. "Wash me throughly from mine iniquity and cleanse me from my sin" (Psalm 51:2). If we want to enjoy the forgiveness David enjoyed, we must quit shifting the blame and start saying, *"my* transgressions," *"mine* iniquity," *"my* sins."

Are you ready to quit shifting the blame?

From Your Heart

What primary truth did you learn from this lesson? Did God bring someone to your mind that could use this lesson? If so, would you be willing to try to share it with him/her?

Notes:

1. Purcell, *Be Still, My Child,* p. 80.

2. Ronald Dunn, *When Heaven Is Silent* (Nashville: Nelson/Word Publishing Group, 1994), p. 158.

3. Purcell, *Be Still, My Child,* p. 138.

4. Jill Briscoe, *Running on Empty* (Dallas: Word Publishing, 1988), p. 52.

5. C. H. Spurgeon, *Morning and Evening* (Lynchburg, VA: The Old-Time Gospel Hour, n.d.), p. 610.

6. Richard Warren, *Answers to Life's Difficult Questions* (Colorado Springs: ChariotVictor Publishing, 1985), p. 27.

Why Cope When You Can Conquer?

Psalm 42

"Why art thou cast down, O my soul? and why art thou disquieted in me? hope thou in God: for I shall yet praise him for the help of his countenance" (Psalm 42:5).

This psalm may have been written by David. It is a psalm of conflicting emotions: sorrow and song, fear and faith, doubt and devotion. David experienced all these emotions in the years when he was running from Saul. He probably wondered at times if God had forgotten him.

David was not the only godly man to experience despondency to the point of depression. Elijah, Moses, and Jonah faced some of these same emotions, as did other great men. Abraham Lincoln knew awful doubt and depression. Charles Haddon Spurgeon, one of the greatest preachers of all times, had a lifetime battle with depression, perhaps partly due to suffering from gout. Winston Churchill, the great English leader, suffered terribly from depression. He said it followed him like a "black dog."

Depression is common in our day as well. The offices of pastors and counselors, doctors and psychiatrists are filled with people suffering from depression. In this lesson we will look at Biblical ways to handle the discouragement and despondency that can lead to depression. If you are depressed, my prayer is that you will get your eyes off your circumstances and onto the Lord, Who can help you regain your hope, confidence, and trust. He will help you move from coping to conquering!

Depression has a number of causes. One of them is *physical exhaustion.* Burnout is common in our rush-rush society, but it is not unique to our time.

1. Elijah may have experienced burnout after the contest on Mount Carmel. After running from Jezebel, he wanted to die. Read 1 Kings 19:4–8. What were Elijah's immediate needs?

"Have you ever felt like a pooped prophet? Perhaps you have been diligently serving the Lord, but just doing too much of everything—running round and round in circles, until eventually you've met yourself coming back. Suddenly it all overwhelms you. If this is the case, watch out! You could end up flat on your face under a broom tree, just like Elijah. It is one thing to be tired 'in' the work of the Lord; it is quite another to be tired 'of' the work itself. There is a difference, you know. When Elijah said, 'I've had it, Lord,' he meant it!"[1]

A second cause of depression is *attacks from Satan.* Satan is our accuser (Revelation 12:10). He knows when to attack us and what weapons to use.

2. (a) Of what does Satan like to remind us?

(b) How can we withstand his attacks? Read Ephesians 6:12–17 and James 4:7.

A third cause of depression is *psychological traits.* All of us are born with different temperaments and personalities. Some people are outgoing and bubbly and always positive and daring. Other people are more withdrawn and quiet and tend to be more negative and gloomy. They may give in to these feelings and develop a pattern of defeat and depression.

One of the most common causes for depression is *discouragement.* That's where we find the psalmist in Psalm 42. Certainly he was in the pit of despair and discouragement, but I don't think he had hit the pit of depression.

3. What do you think is the difference between depression and discouragement? Compare 1 Kings 19:4 and Psalm 42:5.

Psalm 42 is helpful for us because the writer expresses the turmoil going on in his heart and mind. Let's assume the writer was David. At this point in his life, he may have been deprived the privilege of many things he held dear: his home, friends, regular attendance at a place of worship.

Discouragement Can Lead to Despondency (vv. 1–4)
Read Psalm 42:1–4.

4. Read Psalm 42:1 and 2. How was David feeling spiritually? What words give us an indication of his condition?

5. Can you relate to the feelings David experienced? If so, write down what was happening in your life at that time.

" 'The strong are not always vigorous, the wise not always ready, the brave not always courageous, and the joyous not always happy.' Such words were not written in the twentieth century by a compromising pastor or psychologist. They were spoken in the nineteenth century by that 'prince of preachers,' Charles Haddon Spurgeon."[2]

Circumstances can cause us misery, but people can be the real killers. The people in David's life were adding to his misery by sneering at him and asking him, "Where is thy God?" (v. 3).

6. What Scripture verses or thoughts about God can well-meaning friends share that can add to our discouragement rather than help us?

7. David was having a pity party for himself. What words in verse 3 indicate this?

8. We all feel sorry for ourselves occasionally. What can cause a pity party to turn into depression? Read Philippians 3:13.

"When we ask 'What now?' we shift our focus from ourselves to God. . . . Not only does 'what now?' save us from self-pity, but it also gives us something to look forward to. 'What now?' means we are still moving, still growing. In short, we have a future. It means that life can be good again. And this is essential, for there is nothing more bleak than a future that can never be better than the past; nothing more hopeless than believing the best is behind us, that no matter how good life may be, no matter how many good things come to us, life can never be as good as it once was."[3]

---

9. What words in verse 4 indicate David was withdrawing from people and not sharing his hurt with others?

10. Why is it important not to withdraw from others, but to share with others when we are hurting?

The Cure for Despondency (vv. 5–8)
Read Psalm 42:5–8.

11. What was the first thing David did to help himself?

12. David knew God could help him ("Hope thou in God" [v. 5]), but he was still in turmoil. What question might he have been asking God? Read Matthew 27:46. Have you ever asked God questions like this? If so, when?

"In the real world, I struggle against the feeling that, in certain areas of my life, God has forgotten me. Do you struggle with that feeling, too? It's not uncommon. Whether we acknowledge it or not, we all pass through times when life doesn't make sense to us. We do, we dream, we hope, we pray— and still God doesn't fulfill our desires. Why does He keep us waiting? Or why does He sometimes say no? I don't presume to know. But through the years and with hindsight, I'm growing to trust His magnificent wisdom in waiting to change circumstances. And to understand that the greatest miracle is how He changes me while I'm waiting."[4]

---

13. David may or may not have questioned God, but we

know whom he did question. Who was it (v. 5)? What self-talk might he have given himself?

14. (a) What did David start thinking about?

(b) How do you discipline your mind to think on positive thoughts?

15. David still struggled and felt overwhelmed: "All thy waves and thy billows are gone over me" (v. 7), yet he chose to dwell on God rather than on his circumstances. Why do you think David referred to God as "God of my life" in verse 8?

"What does it mean to 'remember the Lord'? . . . What specifically do you remember? Three things. First, remember God's goodness to you in the past. . . . Second, remember God's closeness in the present. . . . Third, remember God's power for the future. . . . Remember, your thoughts determine your feelings. If you are feeling discouraged it's because you are thinking discouraging thoughts. If you want to feel encouraged instead, start thinking encouraging thoughts. Choose some uplifting Bible verses to memorize."[5]

---

16. Sleeplessness often accompanies despondency and depression because people are constantly rehearsing their problems in their minds. (a) What did David do at night (v. 8)?

(b) What could we do to help us calm our souls and go to sleep?

In Case of Relapse (vv. 9–11)
Read Psalm 42:9–11.

17. Sometimes it seems we just get on our feet when we get knocked down again. David was down again (v. 9). Why did he feel God had forgotten him?

18. David asked himself the same question and gave himself the same answer (v. 11). Why didn't David come up with a different answer? Read Psalms 18:1–3 and 23:1.

"Persons who held on in hope, with seemingly little for which to hope, were known to say: 'Then was our mouth filled with laughter . . . We were like them that dream.'"[6]

"In 'hope against hope,' I wait, Lord,
Faced by some fast-barred gate, Lord,
Hope never says 'Too late,' Lord,
Therefore in Thee I hope!

"Hope though the night be long, Lord,
Hope of a glowing dawn, Lord,
Morning must break in song, Lord,
For we are 'saved by hope.'"[7]

19. When your problems overwhelm you and you feel
    yourself sinking, hang on to the promises of God. The
    promises of God are like lifesavers. What are your
    lifesaver verses?

   If you don't have any lifesaver verses, let me tell you
about my "Why Sink When You Can Swim" verses. Several
years ago I compiled this list of verses for my own help and
benefit. These verses were included in my first Bible study
book, *Trials—Don't Resent Them as Intruders.* Since that
time, hundreds of ladies have shared with me how much
these verses have helped them. I hope they will help you.
For those of you old-timers who have been using the verses
for years now, I've added a few new ones (see pages 55 and
56).

 From My Heart
_____

   I don't think I have ever really been in the pit of depression, but I've been close enough to know the feelings of
darkness and loneliness. In my darkest hours I've been able
to give myself a good talking to, as David did, and remind
myself that God is still in control. It is a solid conviction in
my heart that nothing touches my life that God does not
allow. I can get angry at people who hurt me or about miserable circumstances, but ultimately I would have to get angry
with God because He allowed it.

I also remind myself that the ultimate goal of my life is to become more like Jesus Christ—"to be conformed to the image of his Son" (Romans 8:29). God alone knows what dross still has to be removed from life for that process to keep moving forward. James 1:2–4 reminds us not to resent these trials as intruders but to welcome them as friends; they have come to make us more mature spiritually, more like Jesus.

When hard times come, I would encourage you to do what David did to keep yourself out of the pit of depression:

• Self-evaluation—be honest with yourself; admit you are feeling discouraged or depressed, whichever it might be.

• Self-confrontation—talk to yourself; tell yourself to quit reliving your problems and start rehearsing the promises of God.

• Self-discipline—make yourself do what you need to do whether you feel like it or not. Get your trust where it belongs. Get your eyes off your problems and back on the Lord.

If you will do these things, God will put your discouragement or depression where it belongs—in the depths of the sea—and you will conquer rather than merely cope!

From Your Heart

Have you been dwelling on your difficult circumstances instead of the promises of God? Have you been coping rather than conquering? What are you going to change in your life? When are you going to do it? Will you do it today?

Notes:

1. Briscoe, *Running on Empty,* p. 15.

2. Elizabeth Skoglund, *More Than Coping* (Minneapolis: World Wide Publications, 1987), p. 10.

3. Dunn, *When Heaven Is Silent,* p. 80.

4. Judith Couchman, *Lord, Have You Forgotten Me?* (Dallas: Word Publishing, 1992), p. vii.

5. Warren, *Answers to Life's Difficult Questions,* pp. 68, 69.

6. Cowman, *Springs in the Valley,* p. 57.

7. Cowman, *Springs in the Valley,* pp. 57, 58.

WHY SINK WHEN YOU CAN SWIM VERSES

*(Cut this page from your book on the dotted line
and place it in the front of your Bible.)*

Genesis 18:25—"Shall not the Judge of all the earth do right?"

Job 23:10—"But he knoweth the way that I take: when he hath tried me, I shall come forth as gold."

Psalm 18:30—"As for God, his way is perfect: the word of the LORD is tried [proved]: he is a buckler to all those that trust in him."

Psalm 31:15—"My times are in thy hand. . . ."

Psalm 34:4—"I sought the LORD, and he heard me, and delivered me from all my fears."

Psalm 37:23—"The steps of a good man are ordered by the LORD: and he delighteth in his way."

Psalm 46:10—"Be still, and know that I am God."

Psalm 91:1, 2—"He that dwelleth in the secret place of the most High shall abide under the shadow of the Almighty. I will say of the LORD, He is my refuge and my fortress: my God; in him will I trust."

Proverbs 3:5, 6—"Trust in the LORD with all thine heart; and lean not unto thine own understanding. In all thy ways acknowledge him, and he shall direct thy paths."

Proverbs 17:22—"A merry heart doeth good like a medicine: but a broken spirit drieth the bones."

Isaiah 26:3—"Thou wilt keep him in perfect peace, whose mind is stayed on thee: because he trusteth in thee."

Isaiah 40:31—"But they that wait upon the LORD shall renew their strength; they shall mount up with wings as eagles; they shall run, and not be weary; and they shall walk, and not faint."

Isaiah 43:2—"When thou passest through the waters, I will be with thee; and through the rivers, they shall not overflow thee: when thou walkest through the fire, thou shalt not be burned; neither shall the flame kindle upon thee."

Jeremiah 29:11—"For I know the thoughts that I think toward you, saith the LORD, thoughts of peace, and not of evil, to give you an expected end."

Jeremiah 31:3—". . . Yea, I have loved thee with an everlasting love. . . ."

Jeremiah 33:3—"Call unto me, and I will answer thee, and shew thee great and mighty things, which thou knowest not."

Habakkuk 3:17, 18—"Although the fig tree shall not blossom, neither shall fruit be in the vines; the labour of the olive shall fail, and the fields shall yield no meat; the flock shall be cut off from the fold, and there shall be no herd in the stalls: Yet I will rejoice in the LORD, I will joy in the God of my salvation."

Luke 1:37—"For with God nothing shall be impossible."

Romans 8:28, 29—"And we know that all things work together for good to them that love God, to them who are the called according to his purpose. For whom he did foreknow, he also did predestinate to be conformed to the image of his Son, that he might be the firstborn among many brethren."

1 Corinthians 10:13—"There hath no temptation taken you but such as is common to man: but God is faithful, who will not suffer you to be tempted above that ye are able; but will with the temptation also make a way to escape, that ye may be able to bear it."

Philippians 4:4—"Rejoice in the Lord alway: and again I say, Rejoice."

Philippians 4:6, 7—"Be careful [anxious] for nothing; but in every thing by prayer and supplication with thanksgiving let your requests be made known unto God. And the peace of God, which passeth all understanding, shall keep your hearts and minds through Christ Jesus."

Philippians 4:11—"Not that I speak in respect of want: for I have learned, in whatsoever state I am, therewith to be content."

Philippians 4:13—"I can do all things through Christ which strengtheneth me."

Philippians 4:19—"But my God shall supply all your need according to his riches in glory by Christ Jesus."

1 Thessalonians 5:18—"In every thing give thanks: for this is the will of God in Christ Jesus concerning you."

2 Timothy 1:7—"For God hath not given us the spirit of fear; but of power, and of love, and of a sound mind."

Hebrews 13:5—". . . I will never leave thee, nor forsake thee."

James 1:2, 3—"My brethren, count it all joy when ye fall into divers [various] temptations; knowing this, that the trying of your faith worketh patience."

1 Peter 5:7—"Casting all your care upon him; for he careth for you."

Where to Run in Trouble

Psalm 46

*"God is our refuge and strength,
a very present help in trouble" (Psalm 46:1).*

This psalm was written after God intervened in a miraculous way for His people, perhaps when He saved Jerusalem from Sennacherib, the Assyrian conqueror (2 Kings 19; Isaiah 36; 37). His message was, "I am going to destroy Jerusalem." Instead, Sennacherib went home, defeated by God's intervention: 185,000 Assyrians died from a plague by the hand of the angel of the Lord. This song of praise may have been written to remember the victory. It could have been written by Hezekiah, king of Judah, or even Isaiah. The writer is not known, but the message of the psalm is clear: God will be there to help us in the worst of times.

The psalmist had endured such a violent experience it was as if an earthquake had hit and floodwaters were roaring around him. He felt as if everything was shaking and falling apart beneath his feet. Yet he did not sink. How did he survive such an earth-shattering experience and stay on top of things? He had adequate *inward resources* to meet the most extreme *outward circumstances*. He knew where help would come from. It was settled in his heart and mind that the Lord, Who controls Heaven and earth, was on his side. God would never leave him or forsake him: "God is our refuge and strength, a very present help in trouble" (Psalm 46:1).

Martin Luther, who frequently faced danger and death, often felt like David in Psalm 42 when he said, "Why art thou cast down, O my soul?" In those hours Luther would say to his friend, "Come, Philip, let us sing the Forty-sixth Psalm." In 1529 Luther wrote the words and music to the great hymn "A Mighty Fortress Is Our God," based on Psalm 46.

We know God is our refuge, our fortress, our helper, our strength; but do we act like it when an earth-shattering experience hits our lives? I have had some earth-shattering experiences in my life these past few years, and I am learning to "be still" instead of running around in circles when they come. As you study this lesson, my prayer is that you will learn to "be still" and know how great your God is. "Be still, and know that I am God" (Psalm 46:10).

Read Psalm 46.

Verse 1

1. (a) What picture comes to your mind when you think of a refuge?

   (b) When do we need a refuge?

"What assurance is promised us in this verse for time of great need. Life may seem to be going along smoothly. We're happy and contented, serving the Lord, busy with the many things that daily living brings. Then suddenly life changes completely. It seems that everything we hold dear is taken from us. What can we do?. . . Somehow the truth of this verse gets through to us. As we fly to Him, our refuge, we find Him strengthening us to face the future. We may wonder what to do, we may not see our way out, but He reminds us, 'I am—right now, this very moment—your present help.'"[1]

---

2. Sometimes God has to hide us from the storms of life long enough to revive us. What does He use to revive and strengthen us? Read Psalm 119:28 and 105.

3. Christ did not promise us a life without trouble; but what does He want us to do when we are troubled? Read John 14:1.

4. How can the promises of God calm a troubled heart? Read Isaiah 26:3 and 4 and Luke 1:37.

> *"God is present helping us to bear trouble, to improve it, and to survive it. Present by gracious communications and sweet manifestations; present most when he seems absent, restraining, overruling, and sanctifying trouble. Trust and wait."* [2]

5. God is our help in trouble, or tight places.
   (a) What "tight places" have you been in lately when you called upon God to help you?

   (b) Why does God allow these tight places occasionally? Read 1 Peter 1:6–8.

6. In times of trouble the person who is calm is most ready to use the proper means of escape. What means of help can we use in times of trouble? Read Psalm 18:1 and 2.

When God is our REFUGE, STRENGTH, and HELP, we need not FEAR or FAINT because God will FIGHT for us. He works when nothing else works!

Verses 2 and 3

7. Have verses 2 and 3 ever described your life? Have you experienced such a great upheaval that you thought your world was falling apart? If so, explain the situation.

8. When we go through earth-shattering experiences, we will handle them in one of two ways. We will either be filled with nerve-jangling anxiety, or we will be relaxed and peaceful. How can we say, "Therefore will not we fear" when everything is falling apart? Review the account in Exodus 14.

9. The psalmist seemed to be saying, "I will not fear even if the worst thing that could happen does happen." What if the thing you fear most really were to occur in your life? What is the worst thing that could happen? If that happened, what would be the worst result? When you get to the end of your fears, what alternatives do you have? Read Psalm 73:25 and Jonah 1:3.

"I will face my fears, retrace them to their source in my heart, displace them by making my heart Christ's home, and erase them with His perfect love. Face your fears; don't submerge them."[3]

Psalm 46:3 ends with the word "Selah." The psalms are songs, and "Selah" was a pause between stanzas, meaning "think on this." When we see "Selah," we could say, "There, what do you think of that!"

Verses 4 and 5

Most of the great cities in the Bible were located by a river. However, Jerusalem was not. It did not have a river running through it for the city's water supply. In times of war, a city could be cut off from its source of water. But if the source of water was secure, the people felt they could hold out against the enemy. King Hezekiah had built a water system through the rocks to bring water into the city of Jerusalem.

> *"For all his strength and cunning, the enemy knew nothing of this unfailing source of inner refreshment without which the city could not have lasted more than a month or two. . . . The city had a secret river that kept it strong. . . . We have that marvelous river within! The Holy Spirit has come down from the throne of God to fill our hearts and provide us with a deep, unfailing reservoir of spiritual supply. No enemy can stop Him from flowing into us and through us. Let us take fresh note of that when things go wrong."[4]*

10. What was the "city of God" to which the psalmist referred (v. 4)? See also Isaiah 33:20.

11. God dwelled in the midst of His people first in the tabernacle, then in the temple. Because of His presence with them, the people had no reason to shake with fear. Today God the Holy Spirit dwells in us (John 14:17; 1 John 4:2–4). What does the Holy Spirit promise to give us when we are shaking with fear? Read John 14:27 and Philippians 4:7.

12. What is another thing the Holy Spirit wants to do in our lives today? Read John 7:37–39.

13. Describe a time in your life when, humanly speaking, you should have been shaking with fear but you were full of peace.

14. "God shall help her, and that right early" (v. 5). "Right early" can mean "at the turning of the morning." When did the Israelites discover they had been delivered from Sennacherib's invasion (2 Kings 19:35)?

Verses 6, 7, and 11

    As the enemies gathered against the city of God, the nations were in an uproar. Yet the angel of the Lord killed 185,000 Assyrians in one night (2 Kings 19:35). This miraculous event was no big deal to God. He doesn't even tell us how it happened. "Is any thing too hard for the LORD?" (Genesis 18:14).

    "The LORD of hosts is with us" (Psalm 46:7). The same Lord Who was with God's children in Jerusalem is with us today. He Who rules the heavens and all the angels, stars, and planets is with us. He Who rules every person and circumstance on earth is with us. Nothing can touch our lives unless He wills it. "The king's heart is in the hand of the LORD, as the rivers of water: he turneth it whithersoever he will" (Proverbs 21:1).

15. "The God of Jacob is our refuge" (v. 7). What covenant did God make with Jacob? Read Genesis 28:10–15.

16. How do we know God kept His covenant with Jacob? Read Matthew 1:1 and 2.

17. Why is it significant to us that the God of Jacob is our refuge? Read Hebrews 13:5.

"There was something else, however, that occupied the psalmist. There was not only that marvelous river (46:4), there was also the mysterious resident! . . . 'The Lord of hosts is with us; the God of Jacob is our refuge.'. . . We have within also the same mysterious resident who dwelt in Jerusalem so many years ago. . . . The Lord Jesus Himself has come to take up His residence in our hearts and lives. We can shout: 'Emmanuel! God with us! The Lord of hosts is with us, the God of Jacob is our refuge.' Selah! What do you think of that!"[5]

Verses 8 and 9

Commentators suggest that the overthrow of the Assyrian army probably put an end to all the wars being waged at that time. The Assyrian army was the most mighty army on the globe. They had already overrun many of the smaller kingdoms of the world (Isaiah 37:18–20). God had completely overthrown Israel's foe; the Assyrian army was wiped out in one night by the angel of the Lord.

Verse 10

"Be still, and know that I am God" (v. 10) follows the description of God's power in verses 8 and 9. God seems to be saying, "Remember how powerful I am! Slow down long enough to remember Who has control of your life."

18. When earth-shattering experiences rush into our lives, what is often our first response? Read Psalm 106:12 and 13.

> *"It is not too difficult to be cool, calm, and collected when there is nothing to give you a headache. Composure is relatively simple when there is nothing to 'decompose' you. But to be able to react to the unexpected in this unnatural way is difficult. So far as I know, there is only one way of doing it. That is to be so accustomed to being 'still' in the Lord's presence that it becomes an intuitive reaction."[6]*

19. What do the words "know that I am God" (v. 10) mean to you?

20. What plan have you established in your life to get to know God in an intimate way?

21. How will knowing God in a more intimate way help you when the storms of life come?

 ## *From My Heart*

When earth-shaking experiences make me feel like I am slipping and sliding, I always turn to the Psalms. David, who wrote many of the psalms, experienced more ups and downs in his life than any other Bible character I know. Yet no matter how low he would get, he always got up again and soon had a song in his heart. How did he survive all those calamities? He really knew God! He had one driving force in his life: to know God better. "One thing have I desired of the LORD, that will I seek after . . . to behold he beauty of the LORD, and to enquire in his temple" (Psalm 27:4). David was a man after God's own heart (1 Samuel 13:14).

I want to be a lady after God's heart. I want to really know God! I have learned this intimate relationship will not happen overnight. It comes by daily spending time in His presence. I wrote the following words for the preface of my book *Be Still, My Child.*

> "When you truly know how great your God is,
> All your doubts and anxieties will begin to fade;
> When you truly learn to trust His power and might,
> You will never have to fear again.
>
> "He is in control of Heaven and earth;
> He stands ready to work for those who trust Him;
> For those who sincerely believe,
> 'Nothing is impossible with God!'
>
> "He has done all that needs be done to teach you to
>   trust Him;
> He has given you His Holy Spirit to help and
>   strengthen you;
> He lifts you up when you utterly fail;
> He encourages you when you think, 'There's no use
>   trying again.'
> He believes in you; do you believe in Him?
>
> "Do you really know Him well enough to trust Him?
> Slow down; be still!
> Take time in God's presence.
> Then, and only then, will you understand why He said,
> 'Be still, and know that I am God.'"[7]

From Your Heart

What have you learned in this lesson that will help you when you face an earth-shaking experience? How well do you know God? Do you need to know Him better? What are you going to do about it?

Notes:

1. Millie Stamm, *Meditation Moments* (Grand Rapids: Zondervan Publishing House, 1967), August 1.

2. Gray and Adams, *Gray and Adams Bible Commentary,* p. 533.

3. Lloyd Ogilvie, *Turn Your Struggles into Stepping Stones* (Dallas: Word Publishing, 1993), p. 38.

4. John Phillips, *Exploring the Psalms,* vol. 1 (Neptune, NJ: Loizeaux Brothers, 1986), pp. 366, 367.

5. Phillips, *Exploring the Psalms,* vol. 1, pp. 366, 367.

6. Briscoe, *What Works When Life Doesn't,* pp. 155, 156.

7. Purcell, *Be Still, My Child,* p. 10.

Is It Worth It to Be Godly?

Psalm 73

*"For I was envious at the foolish, when I saw
the prosperity of the wicked" (Psalm 73:3).*

Psalm 73 and the following nine psalms were written by Asaph. He was one of the chief musicians appointed by the Levites to lead the music when David brought the ark of the covenant to Jerusalem (1 Chronicles 15:16–19).

The subject addressed in this psalm is the prosperity of the wicked and the suffering of the saints. Asaph struggled with this inequity to the point that he wondered if being godly was really worth all the suffering and sacrifice. Have you ever felt that way? Have you ever thought, "Lord, all I've ever done is try to live a life that pleases You, and this is how You treat me. Is this really fair?" We may not be bold enough to verbalize those words, but I dare say most of us have had similar thoughts.

In this lesson we will be reminded that we can't always have it all; we must choose God or money. "Ye cannot serve God and mammon" (Matthew 6:24). My prayer for you is that you will come to the same conclusion Asaph did: worshiping God is always worthwhile, but riches could lead to ruin.

Read Psalm 73.

Verse 1

1. In verse 1 Asaph stated what he knew was a settled fact; then he shared the emotional upheaval of his feelings in verses 2–28. What was the settled conviction of Asaph's heart?

Verse 2

2. Asaph had worked through some serious doubts and questions about God. How had his doubting affected his life?

3. What are some slippery situations Christians find themselves in where they might begin to doubt God's goodness?

Verse 3

4. (a) Of whom was Asaph envious?

(b) Why would a Christian be envious of proud and prosperous wicked people?

". . . Do not equate wickedness with wealth. Many wealthy people are believers who honor the Lord by using their wealth wisely. It is not wrong to possess money and things, but it is wrong to let money and things possess us."[1]

Verses 4 and 5

5. What two troubles did Asaph think the wicked never had?

Verse 6

6. What else about the wicked troubled Asaph?

Verse 7

7. (a) If we say a person has "more than heart could wish,"
   what do we mean?

   (b) Have you ever looked at someone you know who has
       "more than heart could wish" and felt a little jealous?
       What did that person have that you wished you
       could have?

Verses 8–12

8. In verses 8–12 the psalmist talked about the pride and
   arrogance of the wicked who scoff at the righteous. What
   mocking questions do the wicked ask (v. 11)?

Verses 13 and 14

9. Asaph seemed to be asking, "Why do bad things happen
   to good people and the wicked get off scot-free?" How
   did this envy affect his life?

---

*"The greater the trial, the more intense the pain.
The greater the pain, the more we tend to question
God's purpose. God, however, doesn't fall off His
throne in utter shock when we yell at Him. . . . He
understands, and patiently waits until we have
exhausted our show of bravado. He is not threat-
ened. His caring attitude does not change. He
realizes that the heavenly complaint department*

will always be full of angry callers screaming,
'God is not fair!' "[2]

Verses 15 and 16

10. Of what did Asaph remind himself as he began to see what his envy was doing to himself and what it could do to others?

11. Have you ever been at your wit's end and felt your thoughts were driving you crazy, but you were too embarrassed to let anyone else know how you were feeling? How did you get help?

"Are you standing at 'Wit's End Corner'?
Then you're just in the very spot
To learn the wondrous resources
Of Him who faileth not;
No doubt to a brighter pathway
Your footsteps will soon be moved,
But only at 'Wit's End Corner'
Is the 'God who is able' proved."[3]

Verse 17

12. When Asaph finally came to his senses, he decided to go into the sanctuary (the presence of God) with his problem. How did his thinking change?

"The sanctuary of God may not be in the church.
God's sanctuary for you may be the place of prayer
by your bedside. It may be in the fields, or in an

*automobile. But regardless of place, God's sanctu-
ary for you is the place where your vision is lifted
from the hard-to-understand things of this world to
His eternal purposes."*[4]

Verses 18–20

13. What awaits those who live a wicked life with no time for
    God?

Verse 21

14. How did Asaph express his change of heart?

Verse 22

15. Have you, like Asaph, ever said or done something dumb
    when God seemed unfair? What was it?

Verse 23

16. How is verse 23 similar to Psalm 37:24?

*"How much better to hold hands with God than to
have a hand in every successful business venture
in the world! It is hard for a rich man to let go of his
riches long enough to hold hands with God. . . . No
wonder Jesus said it was easier for a camel to go
through the eye of a needle than for a rich man to
enter Heaven."*[5]

Verse 24

17. What double benefits do believers enjoy according to verse 24?

Verses 25 and 26

18. How did Asaph's focus on life change?

Verse 27

19. What did the psalmist emphasize again in verse 27?

Verse 28

20. Asaph wrestled with the problem of the prosperity of the wicked and came out on top. What was his final conclusion?

21. Relate an experience when you thought God was unfair, but in the end you trusted Him more than you had ever thought you could.

 From My Heart

God is good! Is this a settled conviction in your heart? I have learned through good times and bad times that God is good even when He doesn't seem good. I have also learned that a confident belief in the goodness of God helps me not to listen to Satan when he whispers in my ear, "If God loves you, why is He allowing this to happen to you?" I can't always answer that question, but I do understand everything is under control from God's perspective. Nothing touches my life that God does not allow. Spurgeon's words are a constant encouragement to me: "When you can't trace God's hand, trust His heart."

Asaph was having a hard time seeing God's goodness in his life. It seemed the wicked lived more comfortably and had fewer problems. However, he had forgotten one thing: outward comforts and pleasure do not bring inward comfort and contentment. You cannot buy happiness and peace. Have you been looking with envy and interest at this world and its value system? If so, you had better get your eyes back on God and His value system. Remember, "When you can't trace God's hand, trust His heart." God loves you; *God is good!*

From Your Heart

Is it a settled conviction in your heart that God is good? Where is your "sanctuary" where you come into God's presence each day to be reminded of His goodness to you? If you are having a hard time realizing God is good, write down a different attribute of God each day when you read the Word of God.

Notes:
1. White, *Songs That Touch the Heart,* p. 52.
2. Joel A. Freeman, *God Is Not Fair* (San Bernardino, CA: Here's Life Publishers, 1987), p. 33.
3. Antoinette Wilson, quoted by Mrs. Charles Cowman, *Streams in the Desert,* vol. 1 (Grand Rapids: Zondervan Publishing House), p. 167.
4. Leslie Parrott, quoted by Al Bryant, *Climbing the Heights* (Grand Rapids: Zondervan Publishing House, 1956), April 30.
5. Phillips, *Exploring the Psalms,* vol. 1, pp. 609, 610.

The Blessings of the Secret Place

Psalm 91

"He that dwelleth in the secret place of the most High shall abide under the shadow of the Almighty" (Psalm 91:1).

Psalm 91 is without a title and a known writer; however, the writer may have been Moses. When a writer's name was unknown, Jewish historians assigned the psalm to the last-named writer. In this case, that is Moses, who wrote Psalm 90.

The contents of the entire psalm are condensed into verses 1 and 2: "He that dwelleth in the secret place of the most High shall abide under the shadow of the Almighty. I will say of the LORD, He is my refuge and my fortress: my God; in him will I trust." Verse 1 expresses the safety of the one who places his trust in God. In verse 2 the psalmist expressed his own firm assurance of his safety in Jehovah his God. God was a safe hiding place in the time of trial.

When the heat is on, where do you run for help? Have you learned the safety, security, and serenity of the secret place "under the shadow of the Almighty"? My prayer is that you will learn to enjoy the safe hiding place of the godly, the security of the godly, the blessings of the godly, and the privileges of the godly.

The Safe Hiding Place of the Godly (vv. 1, 2)
Read Psalm 91:1 and 2.

1. Psalm 91 has some tremendous promises, but they are conditional. Who can claim them?

2. What do the words "secret place" in verse 1 indicate?

3. What does it mean to dwell "in the secret place of the most High"? Read John 15:4–11.

4. Those who walk this close to Christ become possessors of rare and special benefits. (a) How do we get close to a person?

(b) How does this relate to walking close to Christ?

5. Read through the psalm and see how many of the rare and special benefits you can find that belong to those who "abide under the shadow of the Almighty." I found fifteen!

6. No protection could be as secure as Jehovah's own shadow. What must we do for someone's shadow to reflect on us?

"The Almighty himself is where his shadow is, and hence those who dwell in his secret place are shielded by himself. What a shade in the day of noxious heat! What a refuge in the hour of deadly storm! Communion with God is safety. The more closely we cling to our Almighty Father the more confident we may be."[1]

---

7. The Almighty is our refuge, our fortress, our God (v. 2).
   (a) What is the difference between a refuge and a fortress as they relate to God's protection?

   (b) Why did the psalmist add "my God"?

The Security of the Godly (vv. 3–10)
Read Psalm 91:3–10.

8. A "fowler" is one who catches small birds, and the "noisome pestilence" refers to disease or woes (v. 3). Who tries to snare, or trap, believers?

9. How does the Lord liken Himself to a bird (v. 4)? Also read Matthew 23:37.

10. Verse 4 gives us a picture of double protection. Since wings and feathers could be broken, what other protection do we have?

11. Not to be afraid of darkness can save us a thousand fears (vv. 5, 6). But Satan also shoots his arrows by day. How could the following verses help those who are fearful of being alone at night or of Satan's attacks? Read Psalms 31:15; 121:4; 139:5–12.

> "... *The man who has sought the mercy seat and is sheltered beneath the wings which overshadow it, shall abide in perfect peace. Days of horror and nights of terror are for other men, his days and nights are alike spent with God, and therefore pass away in sacred quiet. His peace is not a thing of times and seasons, it does not rise and set with the sun, nor does it depend upon the healthiness of the atmosphere or the security of the country. ... Remember that the voice which saith 'thou shalt not fear' is that of God himself, who hereby pledges his word for the safety of those who abide under his shadow, nay, not for their safety only, but for their serenity."*[2]

12. Why did the psalmist feel secure in spite of the evil and "plague" around him (vv. 7–10)?

The Blessings of the Godly (vv. 11–13)
Read Psalm 91:11–13.

13. Only when we get to Heaven will we know what angels did for us (vv. 11, 12). Can you think of a time in your life

when you felt angels were keeping you and bearing you up in their hands? What was it?

"One night I had a dream—
I dreamed I was walking the beach with the
Lord and
Across the sky flashed scenes from my life.
For each scene I noticed two sets of footprints in
the sand,
One belonged to me and the other to the Lord.
When the last scene of my life flashed before us,
I looked back at the footprints in the sand.
I noticed, that many times along the path of my
life,
There was only one set of footprints.
I also noticed that it happened at the very
lowest and saddest times in my life.
This really bothered me and I questioned the
Lord about it.
'Lord, you said that once I decided to follow
you,
You would walk with me all the way,
But I noticed that during the most troublesome
times in my life
There is only one set of footprints.
I don't understand why in times when I needed
you most, you should leave me.'
The Lord replied, 'My precious, precious child, I
love you and I would never, leave you
during your times of trial and suffering.
When you saw only one set of footprints,
It was then that I carried you.'"[3]

---

14. The lion and the adder (or serpent) are pictures of Satan (v. 13). Does this mean that those who walk close to Christ live charmed lives and cannot be touched by Satan? What does it mean? Read Ephesians 6:10–17.

> *"The devil tempts to bring out the worst in us; God permits it so that it might bring out the best. And with every victory gained another step is taken toward the victor's crown."*[4]

The Privileges of the Godly (vv. 14–16)
Read Psalm 91:14–16.

15. The expression "because he hath set his love upon me" (v. 14) indicates a steadfast affection. God's love never changes. What does God expect from His children? Read Matthew 22:37.

16. What does God do for those who fix their love on Him and know His name (v. 14)?

> *"Things look very different according to the standpoint from which we view them. The caterpillar, as it creeps along the ground, must have a widely different 'view' of the world around it from that which the same caterpillar will have when its wings are developed, and it soars in the air above the very places where once it crawled. And similarly the crawling soul must necessarily see things in a very different aspect from the soul that has 'mounted up with wings.' The mountain top may blaze with sunshine when all the valley below is shrouded in fogs, and the bird whose wings can carry him high enough may mount at will out of the gloom below into the joy of the sunlight above."*[5]

17. God always answers prayer (v. 15). What are the three answers He gives?

18. The godly person, whether her life is long or short, is satisfied with her life and content to leave it (v. 16). How has God been weaning you away from this world and making you willing and ready for Heaven?

"Heaven is not here, it's There. If we were given all we wanted here, our hearts would settle for this world rather than the next. God is forever luring us up and away from this one, wooing us to Himself and His still invisible Kingdom, where we will certainly find what we so keenly long for."[6]

 From My Heart

Are you hiding in the shadow of the Savior? I've learned it is a place of safety, security, and serenity. Have you? However, this place of safety, security, and serenity is conditional. Only those who stay close enough to Him to stay in His shadow know it. "He that dwelleth in the secret place of the most High shall abide under the shadow of the Almighty."

Imagine yourself in a desert with the sun beating down, no shade anywhere. No matter where you look, there is no place of relief from the heat of the sun. As far as your eye can see, there is no shelter or trees. As you continue to walk, you find a hidden spot, a place of shade and shadows. There, protected from the heat of the sun, you find relief as long as you stay in the shade of the shelter. Spending time in God's presence (dwelling in the secret place of the most High) is like finding a shaded shelter from the hot sun (under the shadow of the Almighty).

What a privilege to dwell "under the shadow of the Almighty." Do you remember this safe shelter when the heat is on? Are you dwelling in the hot heat or the soothing shadows?

From Your Heart

Where do you go when the heat is on in your life? If you are not close enough to God to be dwelling in His shadow, who moved away: you or God?

Notes:
1. Spurgeon, *The Treasury of David,* vol. 2, p. 89.
2. Spurgeon, *The Treasury of David,* vol. 2, p. 91.
3. Margaret Powers.
4. Phillips, *Exploring the Psalms,* vol. 2, p. 35.
5. Hannah Whitall Smith, *The Christian's Secret of a Happy Life* (Westwood, NJ: Fleming H. Revell Co., 1952), p. 239.
6. Elisabeth Elliot, *Keep a Quiet Heart* (Ann Arbor, MI: Servant Publications, 1995), p. 28.

LESSON 9

God Is Good!

Psalm 100

"For the LORD is good; his mercy is everlasting; and his truth endureth to all generations" (Psalm 100:5).

The message of Psalm 100 is that all the nations of the earth are to worship Jehovah, the God of Israel. They are to come to Jerusalem and enter into the temple courtyards with singing. This song of praise may have been used in a manner similar to this: A group of pilgrims arrived at the outer gates of the temple. They may have come from as far away as Egypt to the west or Mesopotamia to the east. They were met at the gate by an official whose task was to greet them "liturgically." The official asked the pilgrims to turn their backs to the temple. They were to face the nations from which they had just come. In that position, they repeated a command to all the people who dwell on the face of the earth. They shouted to these nations symbolically, "Know ye that the LORD he is God." Then the pilgrims turned around and faced each other. They declared to one another: "It is he that hath made us . . . we are . . . the sheep of his pasture." The official then called out to the people, "Enter into his gates with thanksgiving."

Whether we are serving our family at home, our co-laborers at the office, or in our classroom at church, God has called all believers to the ministry of gladness. "Serve the LORD with gladness." Has serving the Lord become boring, unfulfilling, or drudgery to you? Do you go to church because you know you should, not because you want to? If you have lost your gladness in serving the Lord, Psalm 100 can be a challenging antidote for you.

I pray that as you study this lesson it will be solidly written on your heart forever that God is good! And because He is good, you will serve Him with gladness.

"I saw more clearly than ever that the first great and primary business to which I ought to attend every day was to have my soul happy in the Lord. The first thing to be concerned about was not how much I might serve the Lord, or how I might glorify the Lord, but how I might get my soul into a happy state, and how my inner man might be nourished."[1]

1. Read the above quote by George Mueller again. What can we do each morning to get our souls into a happy state and nourish the inner man? Read Psalm 63:1–5.

2. If your Bible reading has become boring and done out of a sense of duty, try something new. On a sheet of paper, write each letter of the alphabet, A–Z, down the side. As you read your Bible each day, look for an attribute of God or something God is to you to match one of the letters; e.g., A—Almighty; B—Blameless; C—Comforter. What are some other things you could do to add variety to your Bible reading?

Read Psalm 100.

Verse 5

In this psalm we will study verse 5 first. It seems to be the foundation the whole psalm is built on: God is good!

GOD IS GOOD—we can be joyful and serve with gladness (vv. 1, 2).

GOD IS GOOD—we should be conscious of His sovereignty (v. 3).

GOD IS GOOD—we should have an attitude of gratitude (v. 4).

One person suggested we look at the psalm as a song with three stanzas and verse 5 as the chorus to be sung after each stanza.

3. Read the first five words in verse 5. When do we often use these words?

4. When are we less likely to speak these words?

I have a plaque in my home that constantly reminds me of God's goodness. It reads: "Your heavenly Father is too good to be unkind and too wise to make a mistake."[2]

5. Why is it necessary to *always* believe that God is *always* good? Read John 15:11.

6. How would you compare the way you show mercy with the way God shows mercy?

"Justice without mercy is cold-blooded. Justice follows the letter of the law, mercy lets us read between the lines. And there are more extenuating circumstances between the lines than cruel, vengeful people can see. Cold bloody eyes see only the decree's cold, hard type. Have a heart. Season justice with compassion. We are not apt to get what we don't give. Sooner or later we will be needing a little leniency. Justice could be final; but a touch of humanity will give us another chance."[3]

---

7. God says what He means and means what He says. He says, "His truth endureth" (v. 5). What are some situations in which man's "truth" does not endure?

GOD IS GOOD—we can be joyful and serve with gladness (vv. 1, 2)

8. What does it mean to "make a joyful noise unto the LORD"?

9. Believers are called to the ministry of gladness. We have the joyous opportunity to give hope and healing to others. How could majoring on speaking cheerful words to others be making a "joyful noise unto the LORD"? Read Colossians 3:23.

"There is truth to that Japanese saying 'One kind word can warm up three winter months.' Even Mark Twain, not known to be a very vain man, once confessed that he could live three weeks on a compliment."[4]

Proverbs 12:25 says, "Heaviness in the heart of man maketh it stoop: but a good word maketh it glad." Later Solomon wrote, "Pleasant words are as an honeycomb, sweet to the soul, and health to the bones" (Proverbs 16:24). Jeanne Doering says that friends who speak like this are like "bottled sunshine."

10. The true motive for gladness in serving the Lord is gratitude for God's goodness. What will happen to us if we are serving the Lord for human recognition and affirmation? Read Matthew 6:5.

11. How can changing the focus of why we serve change our attitude in service? Read Colossians 3:23 and 24.

"But what if we don't happen to feel glad? My response is, let's fight our way through our moods to gladness. Gloomy moods are a symptom of a need for fresh grace. Let's ask the Lord for a renewed experience of His love and forgiveness, and that will be the first step to gladness. Unpleasant moods are a projection of what's on our minds and in our hearts. Often they are the result of feeling neglected, hurt, or misunderstood, or they fester in the mire of unexpressed feelings about what life has done or failed to do for us. We are Christ's people, called to resign from the 'me generation.' We have been commissioned to be channels of joy and hope. The undeniable test of our Christianity is that we are identified by a contagious gladness."[5]

GOD IS GOOD—we should be conscious of His sovereignty (v. 3)

12. What does this statement mean: "the LORD he is God"? Read Isaiah 45:5–7; Psalms 135:6; 115:3.

13. God is the potter, and we are the clay. He fashions us as He chooses (Jeremiah 1:5; Psalm 139:13–16). What do you like about yourself? What is there about your body or personality you wish God had made differently?

" 'Lord, thank You for making me a unique, one-of-a-kind creation. It is overwhelming to realize there is no one else in this whole world just exactly like me. No one else has fingerprints just like mine; no one else acts just like me. Lord, don't You ever run out of ideas?

'Lord, thank You for creating me with a plan for my life. Before I was ever born, You planned for me to be like Your Son. You want me to be a reflection of Christ on this earth. Lord, only You would set such high expectations for Your children. Had I planned my life, I would just be drifting aimlessly.

'Lord, thank You for making me feel so special! You are my Elohim—my Creator; I was made in Your image. You have chosen me; You told me I have infinite, eternal value. Wow! Am I special! No longer do I have to search for significance; I am significant in Your sight!' "[6]

---

14. God fashions our bodies as He chooses. He also fashions the circumstances He allows in our lives. Romans 8:28 says that, for believers, all our circumstances are fashioned for our good. Where must our focus be in order to see all circumstances as good for us? Read Romans 8:29.

15. God calls us His "people" and "the sheep of his pasture." How do these names remind us of His sovereign control in our lives? Read Isaiah 30:21.

16. (a) Why do sheep need someone to guide them?

(b) How are we like sheep? Read Isaiah 53:6.

GOD IS GOOD—we should have an attitude of gratitude (v. 4)

17. When you think of God's goodness to you, what are some things for which you are most grateful?

18. Finish this statement: It is a settled conviction in my life that God is good because _____

_____

 From My Heart

_____

"God is too good to be unkind and too wise to make a mistake." Many things have happened in my life that I do not understand. However, I have learned that God does not ask me to understand but to accept and trust. He says to me, "What I do thou knowest not now; but thou shalt know hereafter" (John 13:7).

God is good; He loves me; His loving heart directs His hand. If I can trust His heart, I need not question His hand. They will never contradict each other.

I once read the following on a plaque: "I believe in the sun when it does not shine. I believe in God when He is silent. I know the sun is up there even on the darkest day. And when darkness veils Jesus' face, I rest on His unchanging grace."

My heart echoes, "Amen!" God is good!

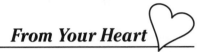

From Your Heart

Have you been doubting God's goodness? How has God been teaching you that He is good? When is the last time you told someone else about the goodness of God?

Notes:

1. George Mueller.

2. Attributed to Robert Ketcham. This plaque is available from Regular Baptist Press. It is printed on heavy ivory parchment paper; 8" x 6" unframed. Call 1-800-727-4440 to order copies of RBP5523; or contact your distributor.

3. Leroy Brownlow, *Thoughts of God* (Fort Worth: Brownlow Publishing Co., 1990), p. 60.

4. Jeanne Doering, *The Power of Encouragement* (Chicago: Moody Press, 1982), p. 39.

5. Ogilvie, *Falling into Greatness,* pp. 163, 164.

6. Purcell, *Be Still, My Child,* p. 352.

Forgetting What We Should Remember

Psalm 106:1–18

*"Then believed they his words; they sang his praise.
They soon forgat his works; they waited not
for his counsel" (Psalm 106:12, 13).*

The Hebrew hymnbook, another title for the book of
Psalms, contains three psalms that give a lengthy record of
Israel's history: Psalms 78, 105, and 106. Psalms 105 and 106
are companion psalms. Psalm 105 tells how God treated
Israel, and Psalm 106 tells how Israel treated God. One
psalm deals with God's faithfulness and the other with
Israel's unfaithfulness.

If the Hebrew people were to remember their history, it
had to be done through word and song since books were
beyond the reach of ordinary people. Psalm 105 starts with
these words: "O give thanks unto the LORD; call upon his
name: make known his deeds among the people. Sing unto
him, sing psalms unto him: talk ye of all his wondrous
works" (vv. 1, 2). What a way to have a history lesson—
through song.

There is an uncertainty about the writer of Psalm 106,
however some commentators think it could be David. This
assumption is based on the fact that verses 1, 47, and 48 are
found in David's writings in 1 Chronicles 16:34–36.

As we study this lesson, we will be amazed at God's
faithfulness and mercy to this rebellious and ungrateful
people. My prayer is that we will see how often we act like
these complaining, murmuring children of God who forgot
so quickly what God wanted them to remember. Let's open
our hearts and be ready to make the necessary changes in
our lives.

Praise and Prayer (vv. 1–5)
Read Psalm 106:1–5.

1. No one had more reason to praise God for His goodness
   and mercy than the Children of Israel. Why? Read Psalm
   106:1, 6, and 7.

2. The psalmist asked the question, "Who can utter the
   mighty acts of the LORD? who can shew forth all his
   praise?" Only when we have experienced the mighty acts
   of God can we utter praises to Him. Make a list of some
   of the mighty acts of God in your life since the day of
   your salvation.

3. The psalmist knew the way to happiness was simple, but
   it was not easy for sinners who were constantly prone
   toward folly and iniquity. Who enjoys the blessed, happy
   life (v. 3)?

4. The psalmist knew the people didn't deserve God's favor
   again because of their sin, but he knew God was
   merciful; so he asked for deliverance. How does this
   relate to us today? Read 1 John 1:9.

"Israel's sins could not exhaust the lovingkind-
ness of God. Neither can ours. Though we forget
Him, He does not forget us; though we turn to our
own ways and leave Him out in the cold, His

> *lovingkindness pursues us. He is the love which
> 'will not let me go,' the love that the many waters
> cannot quench, the love that conquers death."[1]*

5. In verse 5 three different names are used for Israel. What are they?

Israel's Sin in Egypt and at the Red Sea (vv. 6–12)
Read Psalm 106:6–12.

6. The psalmist used three word pictures to describe the condition of the people (v. 6). What are they?

7. Look up the following words in a Bible dictionary or a regular dictionary and write their meaning.

Sin

Iniquity

Wickedness

8. What miracles had the Children of Israel seen in Egypt before they got to the Red Sea, where God worked another miracle (Exodus 7—11)? What miracle did God perform in each of the ten plagues?

Exodus 7:19—(1) plague of blood

Exodus 8:5, 6—(2) plague of frogs

Exodus 8:16, 17—(3) plague of lice

Exodus 8:21, 24—(4) plague of flies

Exodus 9:3, 6—(5) plague of animal disease

Exodus 9:8, 9—(6) plague of boils

Exodus 9:18, 22–26—(7) plague of hail

Exodus 10:4, 13, 14—(8) plague of locusts

Exodus 10:21, 22—(9) plague of darkness

Exodus 11:4–7; 12:3, 7, 12–14—(10) plague of the first-born

9. The plagues ended with a memorial service, described in Exodus 12. What did God want the Children of Israel to remember? Read Exodus 12:23–28.

10. In spite of the ten plagues God sent on Pharaoh's land, Pharaoh would not free the Israelites from his tyranny. In Exodus 13 God freed the Israelites and led them out of the land of Egypt for the Promised Land, by way of the Red Sea. Psalm 106:7 says the Israelites "provoked" God at the Red Sea. How did they do this? Read Exodus 14:10–12.

"How often God must be grieved with us, too, for our persistent unbelief in the face of all He has done for us. Just let a crisis or a difficulty arise, and back we go to our unbelief. It is well enough for us to sing once the difficulty has passed, but why can we not sing and praise God, looking to Him in the midst of difficulty, knowing that it is but another opportunity for us to see Him at work?"[2]

---

11. How did God show undeserved favor to His ungrateful children at the Red Sea? Read Exodus 14:13–16 and Psalm 106:8–10.

12. How did God save them "from the hand of him that hated them" (Psalm 106:10)? Read Exodus 14:24–30.

13. What was the Israelites' reaction after God saved them? Read Exodus 15:1–21 and Psalm 106:12.

14. How do we often imitate the actions of the Israelites at the Red Sea?

Lusting in the Wilderness (vv. 13–15)
Read Psalm 106:13–15.

15. You would think the Israelites would never forget God's faithfulness to them. What happened three days after God's miraculous deliverance at the Red Sea? Read Exodus 15:22–24.

"Continuance in sin and continuance in unbelief go hand in hand. If the people had believed God, they would not have continued to sin; and if they had not continued to sin, they would have believed God. Can a believer live in unbelief? I think so. When I disobey God and live in rebellion against Him, it is as if I am saying to Him, 'I know what your Word says, but I don't want to believe it. I'll just pretend like I never heard it.' I choose to live like an ungrateful, rebellious, spoiled brat. Hebrews 10:31 says, 'It is a fearful thing to fall into the hands of the living God.' The Children of Israel paid for their rebellion, and we will too."[3]

16. How long was it before the Israelites were complaining again, and about what did they complain? Read Exodus 16:1–3.

17. God provided manna every day for the people to eat (Exodus 16:4–7). But the people weren't satisfied.
    (a) What else did they want (Numbers 11:4–13)?

    (b) When they got it, did it satisfy them (Numbers 11:31–33; Psalm 106:15)?

18. When we insist on having our own way, how can God send leanness to our souls? See, for example, the account in Luke 15:11–24.

"To gain silver and lose gold is a poor increase; but to win for the body and lose for the soul is far worse. How earnestly might Israel have unprayed her prayers had she known what would come with their answer! The prayers of lust will have to be wept over. We fret and fume till we have our desire, and then we have to fret still more because the attainment of it ends in bitter disappointment."[4]

Envying Moses and Aaron (vv. 16–18)
Read Psalm 106:16–18.

19. In Numbers 16:1–3 we read that Korah, Dathan, and Abiram led a rebellion against Moses and Aaron. They felt they were as qualified as Moses and Aaron to be Israel's leaders. (a) How did God judge them? Read Numbers 16:31–33 and Psalm 106:17.

(b) What happened to the 250 men who followed their
leadership (Numbers 16:34, 35; Psalm 106:18)?

20. What does this vivid account teach us? Read Psalm
105:15 and 2 Samuel 1:14.

From My Heart

One would think the Israelites would never forget what
God did at the Red Sea. He parted the water so they could
walk through on dry ground; then He brought the water
back together when the Egyptians started across. How long
did they sing God's praises and remember this great
miracle? Only three days! Can you believe that? Three days
later they were complaining and murmuring against God.

I am embarrassed to admit it, but I often act like the
Children of Israel. I forget what I should remember and
remember what I should forget. After all the wonderful
things God has done for me, you would think I would always
be full of faith and never fear any situation I have to face.
But I still find myself asking, What if this happens? How will
this ever work out? Why doesn't God show me what I should
do? I forget so soon that God is in control of all my "what
if's," "how's," and "why's." He will show me what I need to
know when I need to know it!

From Your Heart

What did God teach you about yourself in this lesson?
Are there any similarities in your life when you look at the
Children of Israel? What is the most obvious sin God put His
finger on in your life? What are you going to do about it?

Notes:
1. Phillips, *Exploring the Psalms,* vol. 2, p. 153.
2. Phillips, *Exploring the Psalms,* vol. 2, p. 156.
3. Purcell, *Be Still, My Child,* p. 206.
4. Spurgeon, *The Treasury of David,* vol. 2, p. 367.

LESSON 11

Remembering What We Should Forget

Psalm 106:19–48

"They made a calf in Horeb, and worshipped the molten image. . . .They forgat God their saviour, which had done great things in Egypt" (Psalm 106:19, 21).

The Children of Israel had been out of Egypt for three months. Moses was preparing to meet with God on Mount Sinai (Exodus 19:1–6). Moses called the people together and told them what he was going to do. What was their response? "And all the people answered together, and said, All that the LORD hath spoken we will do. And Moses returned the words of the people unto the LORD" (Exodus 19:8).

But in the very place where they had solemnly vowed to obey God, the Israelites boldly violated the first two commandments: "Thou shalt have no other gods before me. Thou shalt not make unto thee any graven image, or any likeness of any thing that is in heaven above, or that is in the earth beneath, or that is in the water under the earth" (Exodus 20:3, 4).

While Moses was on the mountain with God, the people made a graven image, a golden calf. But it was worse than that! They worshiped the image! Instead of remembering all the wondrous things God had done for them, they were remembering what they should have forgotten—Egypt.

As we move through this lesson, we will be amazed over and over again at Israel's sinfulness and God's mercy and faithfulness to His people. My prayer is that we will be reminded how easy it is to go astray when we start looking at the world instead of keeping our eyes fixed on our great God.

The Golden Calf (vv. 19–23)
Read Psalm 106:19–23.

97

1. Where did the Israelites get the idea to make a golden calf to worship? Read Exodus 32:1–4.

2. The Israelites had forgotten Moses and God. After everything God had done for them, what were they saying (Exodus 32:4)?

3. How does the Israelites' constant yearning for the things they had in Egypt remind us of ourselves?

4. Read Psalm 106:21 and 22. Have you ever been like the Israelites and forgotten God's faithfulness to you?

5. To what extent would God have destroyed His Chosen People (Psalm 106:23) had not Moses interceded for them? Read Exodus 32:7–10.

"Behold the power of a righteous man's intercession. Mighty as was the sin of Israel to provoke vengeance, prayer was mightier in turning it away. How diligently ought we to plead with the Lord for this guilty world, and especially for his own backsliding people! Who would not employ an agency so powerful for an end so gracious! The Lord still hearkens to the voice of a man, shall not our voices be often exercised in supplicating for a guilty people?"[1]

---

6. Psalm 106:24 says the people "despised" the land God was giving them. How did they do this? Read Numbers 13:1–3, 17, 25–33 and 14:1–4.

7. How did God chastise the people for their unbelief? Read Numbers 14:26–30.

8. Why did God allow Joshua and Caleb to go into the land? Read Numbers 14:6–10.

"At Kadesh-Barnea they trembled with fear
And they canceled the journey they'd planned;
For the spies they had sent gave an evil report
Of the giants that dwelt in the land.

" 'They live in the mountains and we are, indeed
Like grasshoppers in their sight.
They are so tall, and we are so small,
It's foolish to think we can fight!'

"Poor Caleb and Joshua try as they might
Could not seem to get them to hear;
'We're able!' they cried, 'In the strength of the Lord
We can conquer, so let us not fear!' . . .

"Oh, God! When I meet the great giants of doubt
Lest to fear and dismay I should yield
May the spirit of Caleb and Joshua rise
To remind me that you are my shield.

"And let me by faith claim your promise to me
And the land that you said should be mine;
Let me plant my feet firmly on each foot of ground
As you lead by your power divine."[2]

9. How does the Israelites' unbelief compare to our hesitancy to undertake something new; e.g., a new job, a move to a new location? Read Proverbs 3:5 and 6 and Psalm 37:23.

The Worship of Baal (vv. 28–31)
Read Psalm 106:28–31.

10. Why did God send the plague (mentioned in Psalm 106:29) upon His people? Read Psalm 106:28–30 and Numbers 25:1–9.

11. (a) How many people died in the plague (Numbers 25:9)?

    (b) Whom did God use to stop the plague (Numbers 25:7–11)?

The Water of Meribah (vv. 32, 33)
Read Psalm 106:32 and 33.

12. How did the Israelites persistent rebellion, faultfinding, and unbelief affect their leader Moses? Read Numbers 20:7–12.

13. What does this account teach us in regard to our pastors and other spiritual leaders?

> "Moses was at last wearied out, and began to grow angry with them, and utterly hopeless of their ever improving; can we wonder at it, for he was man and not God? After forty years bearing with them the meek man's temper gave way, and he called them rebels, and showed unhallowed anger; and therefore he was not permitted to enter the land which he desired to inherit. Truly, he had a sight of the goodly country from the top of Pisgah, but entrance was denied him, and thus it went ill with him. It was their sin which angered him, but he had to bear the consequences; however clear it may be that others are more guilty than ourselves, we should always remember that this will not screen us, but every man must bear his own burden."[3]

Failure in Canaan (vv. 34–43)
Read Psalm 106:34–43.

14. Why did God command the Children of Israel to destroy the nations in Canaan, the Promised Land? Read Deuteronomy 7:1–6.

15. The Israelites did not exterminate the wickedness from the land as God had told them to do. It wasn't long until they were as wicked as those whom they were told to destroy (Psalm 106:39). What does this teach us?

16. How did God feel about the defiant disobedience of His children (Psalm 106:40)?

17. What happened as a result of the people's disobedience (Psalm 106:41, 42)?

God's Faithfulness (vv. 44–48)

Read Psalm 106:44–48.

18. How did God demonstrate His everlasting love to His
    people (Psalm 106:44–46)?

---

*"Notwithstanding all these provoking rebellions
and detestable enormities the Lord still heard
their prayer and pitied them. This is very wonderful, very godlike. One would have thought that the
Lord would have shut out their prayer, seeing they
had shut their ears against his admonitions; but
no, he had a father's heart, and a sight of their
sorrows touched his soul, the sound of their cries
overcame his heart, and he looked upon them
with compassion. His fiercest wrath towards his
own people is only a temporary flame, but his love
burns on for ever like the light of his own immor-
tality."[4]*

---

19. Why did the psalmist ask God to deliver His people from
    their captives (Psalm 106:47, 48)?

The Israelites were weary of the ways of the ungodly
nations who had taken them captive; they longed to be
brought back into their own land where they could worship
Jehovah God. Weaned from their idols, they longed to make
mention of Jehovah's mercies and faithfulness to them.
They wanted to render their gratitude to the One Who had
saved them.

20. Some people profess to be God's children, but they
    continue to live in sin and rebellion. What does God say
    about these people? Read 1 John 2:19.

From My Heart

Moses should be a constant reminder to us that it is not how we start but how we finish that people will remember. How sad it is when one who has walked close to God and run the race well stumbles within a few steps of the final goal.

Moses had put up with the murmuring, complaining Children of Israel for forty years; just a few months more and they would cross the Jordan and enter the Promised Land. But he didn't rule his spirit, and he lost the privilege of entering the land. He had ruled the people all those years, but he was no longer master of himself. He could blame others for his sin—and surely they did provoke him—but he was responsible before God for his actions. We cannot blame others for our sin. We each have to discipline and control our own body, emotions, and spirit. No one can do it for us. We all need to be on guard that we don't allow Satan trip us up when we are tired and provoked with others.

"Set a watch, O LORD, before my mouth; keep the door of my lips" (Psalm 141:3). "Lord, that is my prayer as well; keep me from 'presumptuous sins' (Psalm 19:13) that I might finish well and not be an embarrassment to You."

From Your Heart

Do you tend to remember what you should forget? Do you have things from your pre-conversion years that you need to get rid of? Has God put His finger on some area of rebellion, critical spirit, or unbelief in your life? What are you going to do about it?

Notes:
1. Spurgeon, *The Treasury of David,* vol. 2., p. 369.
2. Joyce Hart, *Mount up with Wings* (published by Joyce Hart, 1998), p. 28.
3. Spurgeon, *The Treasury of David,* vol. 2, pp. 371, 372.
4. Spurgeon, *The Treasury of David,* vol. 2, p. 374.

In God's Sight

Psalm 139

"Whither shall I go from thy spirit? or whither shall I flee from thy presence?" (Psalm 139:7).

Psalm 139 was written by David, perhaps when he was running from his enemies. (Verses 19–22 would seem to indicate that situation.) David knew that no matter what his enemies did or what circumstances he faced, God was right there with him. God knew everything David was thinking and feeling about his situation. David opened himself before God: "Search me, O God, and know my heart: try me, and know my thoughts" (v. 23).

This psalm extols God's omniscience, omnipresence, omnipotence, and righteousness. Man is surrounded by God, pervaded by His Spirit, and unable to take a step without His control. God is our judge and our friend. We are to love Him and fear Him. My prayer is that you will understand yourself and God better after studying this lesson.

1. Look up the following words and write a brief definition of each one.

Omniscient

Omnipresent

Omnipotent

Righteous

God's Omniscience (vv. 1–6)
Read Psalm 139:1–6.

2. David summarized God's omniscience in verse 1 and then described it more fully in the following verses. Write verse 1 in your own words.

"God is not spying on people, trying to catch them in a fault, but He is omniscient, meaning that He knows all things. David found that truth comforting, not frightening (Psalm 139:1–6). He recognized that God knew his life from the time he got up in the morning to the time he lay down at night. God knew his thoughts, and even before he spoke a word, God knew what it would be. . . . What is the significance of this? For the believer it is a great comfort. Nothing happens to you that escapes the notice of your Father. He who sees the sparrow fall from the tree also sees your grief."[1]

---

3. Other people cannot see the intent of our hearts, and yet they judge us. They misjudge our public attitudes and actions as well as our private, quiet lives. We will never have to fear this will happen with God. Why? Read Psalm 139:2 and 3 and Hebrews 4:12.

4. We don't have to be transparent with God because He already knows everything we are thinking and feeling.

What does it mean to be transparent with people? Why is it helpful to be transparent with others occasionally?

5. David said God "beset me behind and before" (v. 5). God had shut him in, or put a hedge around him, and kept His hand on him. What does it mean for God to put a hedge about us? Read Job 1:10.

6. When David realized how intimately God knew him, the thought of it all was overwhelming (v. 6). Why should the thought of God's omniscience fill us with awe and courage?

God's Omnipresence (vv. 7–12)
Read Psalm 139:7–12.

We cannot hide from God because He is omniscient. We cannot be separated from God because He is omnipresent; He is everywhere.

> " 'Whither shall I go from thy spirit?' Not that the Psalmist wished to go from God, or to avoid the power of the divine life; but he asks this question to set forth the fact that no one can escape from the all-pervading being and observation of the Great Invisible Spirit. . . . This makes it dreadful work to sin; for we offend the Almighty to his face, and commit acts of treason at the very foot of his throne. Go from him, or flee from him we cannot: neither by patient travel nor by hasty flight can we

> *withdraw from the all-surrounding Deity. His mind is in our mind; himself within ourselves. His spirit is over our spirit; our presence is ever in his presence."*[2]

7. What does God's hand do for the believer (v. 10)?

8. Why would a believer want to flee from God, Who is both light and love?

God's Omnipotence (vv. 13–18)
Read Psalm 139:13–18.

9. To understand verse 13, we need to know what the words "possessed," "reins," and "covered" mean. Look in the column references of your Bible or a Bible dictionary to find the definitions.

10. Write verse 13 in your own words.

11. To adequately praise God for the way we are "fearfully and wonderfully made" (v. 14), we need to understand human anatomy. Describe just one part of your body that you know is fearfully and wonderfully made.

> *"Do you understand all that God does to keep your body working right day after day? Thousands of things have to work together simultaneously. Consider these facts about the complexity of the heart alone. At rest, the heart pumps about 2 ounces of blood per beat, making a total of 5 quarts per minute! The heart contracts, or beats, 4,000 or more times an hour. So every hour over 300 quarts of blood pass through the heart. Other parts of the body are just as complex and just as amazing."[3]*

12. No two human beings are exactly alike, and no two people have the same fingerprints. How can that be?

13. Why do you think the psalmist compared God's thoughts toward him to the sand of the sea (vv. 17, 18)?

14. What kind of thoughts, or plans, does God have for His children? Read Jeremiah 29:11.

God's Righteousness (vv. 19–24)
Read Psalm 139:19–24.

15. Why did the psalmist abruptly change from praise to vengeance (vv. 19, 20)?

16. David hated those who hated God. Yet he said it was a perfect hatred (v. 22). What did he mean?

17. How do we know David had no desire for personal vengeance against his enemies (v. 23)?

18. We know God searches our hearts whether we ask Him to or not. When might we pray this type of prayer?

"There is no one present who has not a history. There are facts in every life, perhaps, which we would not tell to those nearest and dearest to us. There have been sins cherished in the heart, if not practised in the life. There are secrets unrevealed, scarcely, perhaps, remembered, seldom dwelt upon; but there is a history in each one of us. Now, the Word of God has a wonderful power of fastening upon some critical point in that history, so as to detect the evil—to lay bare the secret—to drag it out, as it were, into the light, and, letting the light of truth shine in upon it, to lead the man to know himself."[4]

---

19. How can we do exploratory surgery for sin in our lives each day? Read Hebrews 4:12.

 From My Heart

Have you ever tried to run away from God? Jonah did. How foolish of Jonah to think that God would be in Nineveh but not in Tarshish. Jonah tried to run away from the presence of God and ended up in the belly of a whale. Even there, God knew exactly where His runaway servant was (Jonah 1).

I remember a time in my life when I tried to run away from God. What a miserable five years. God would not let me alone. I, like Jonah, didn't want to serve God. I didn't want to be a preacher's wife; I wasn't going to be a preacher's wife! God almost had to kill me, like He did Jonah, to change my mind. Finally I fell on my knees before God; I was ready to surrender my will to do His will. That was the wisest decision I have ever made. I am so glad there was no place to go where I could flee from His presence!

From Your Heart

Have you been trying to run from God? Does it comfort you or frighten you to know that around every corner you turn you will face God? How has this lesson helped you see the greatness of God and the uniqueness of each person He creates?

Notes:

1. Paul Enns, *Approaching God* (Chicago: Moody Press, 1991), January 14.

2. Spurgeon, *The Treasury of David,* vol. 3, p. 260.

3. Purcell, *Be Still, My Child,* p. 353.

4. William Jones, *Homiletic Commentary on the Book of Psalms,* vol. 2 (New York: Funk & Wagnalls Co., 1892), p. 390.

LEADER'S
GUIDE

Suggestions for Leaders

The effectiveness of a group Bible study usually depends on two things: (1) the leader herself; and (2) the ladies' commitment to prepare beforehand and interact during the study. You cannot totally control the second factor, but you have total control over the first one. These brief suggestions will help you be an effective Bible study leader.

You will want to prepare each lesson a week in advance. During the week, read supplemental material and look for illustrations in the everyday events of your life as well as in the lives of others.

Encourage the ladies in the Bible study to complete each lesson before the meeting itself. This preparation will make the discussion more interesting. You can suggest that ladies answer two or three questions a day as part of their daily Bible reading time rather than trying to do the entire lesson at one sitting.

You may also want to encourage the ladies to memorize the key verse for each lesson. (This is the verse that is printed in italics at the start of each lesson.) If possible, print the verses on 3" x 5" cards to distribute each week. If you cannot do this, suggest that the ladies make their own cards and keep them in a prominent place throughout the week.

The physical setting in which you meet will have some bearing on the study itself. An informal circle of chairs, chairs around a table, someone's living room or family room—these types of settings encourage people to relax and participate. In addition to an informal setting, create an atmosphere in which ladies feel free to participate and be themselves.

During the discussion time, here are a few things to observe.

• Don't do all the talking. This study is not designed to be a lecture.

• Encourage discussion on each question by adding ideas and questions.

• Don't discuss controversial issues that will divide the group. (Differences of opinion are healthy; divisions are not.)

• Don't allow one lady to dominate the discussion. Use statements such as these to draw others into the study: "Let's hear from someone on this side of the room" (the side opposite the dominant talker); "Let's hear from someone who has not shared yet today."

• Stay on the subject. The tendency toward tangents is always possible in a discussion. One of your responsibilities as the leader is to keep the group on track.

• Don't get bogged down on a question that interests only one person.

You may want to use the last fifteen minutes of the scheduled time for prayer. If you have a large group of ladies, divide into smaller groups for prayer. You could call this the "Share and Care Time."

If you have a morning Bible study, encourage the ladies to go out for lunch with someone else from time to time. This is a good way to get acquainted with new ladies. Occasionally you could plan a time when ladies bring their own lunches or salads to share and eat together. These things help promote fellowship and friendship in the group.

The formats that follow are suggestions only. You can plan your own format, use one of these, or adapt one of these to your needs.

2-hour Bible Study

10:00—10:15 Coffee and fellowship time
10:15—10:30 Get-acquainted time
Have two ladies take five minutes each to tell something about themselves and their families.
Also use this time to make announcements and, if appropriate, take an offering for the baby-sitters.
10:30—11:45 Bible study
Leader guides discussion of the questions in the day's lesson.
11:45—12:00 Prayer time

2-hour Bible Study

10:00—10:45 Bible lesson
Leader teaches a lesson on the content of the material. No discussion during this time.
10:45—11:00 Coffee and fellowship
11:00—11:45 Discussion time
Divide into small groups with an appointed leader for each group. Discuss the questions in the day's lesson.
11:45—12:00 Prayer time

1¹/₂-hour Bible Study

10:00—10:30 Bible study
Leader guides discussion of half the questions in the day's lesson.
10:30—10:45 Coffee and fellowship
10:45—11:15 Bible study
Leader continues discussion of the questions in the day's lesson.
11:15—11:30 Prayer time

ANSWERS FOR LEADER'S USE

Information inside parentheses ( ) is additional instruction for the group leader.

LESSON 1

1. They are looking to people and circumstances to give them happiness.

2. If counsel is not based on Scriptural principles, it is based on man's ideas and philosophies. Man's ideas usually take us down a dead-end street away from God.

3. He might begin to accept the way they walk and talk by accepting their lifestyle and their way of reasoning.

4. The law of the Lord is God's Word. It tells us what we should and should not do and what will happen if we obey and what we can expect if we don't.

5. This person finds pleasure in reading and obeying the Word of God.

6. By carefully reading the Word and then pondering the thoughts you have read throughout the day. A casual glance is not enough to enrich your soul and bring joy to your heart.

7. (Ask some of the ladies to share what they do for their devotional time.)

8. "Planted": strong; "bringeth forth his fruit": productive; "shall not wither": perseveres; "shall prosper": prosperous.

9. (a) Our source of strength is the Lord. His Spirit, like a river of water, strengthens our mind, will, and emotions. (b) The happy Christian is like a tree whose roots go deep; there is great stability in the life.

10. Spiritual fruit: love, joy, peace, long-suffering, gentleness, goodness, faithfulness, meekness, and self-control.

11. When patience is needed to endure, the Christian brings forth the fruit of long-suffering. She brings forth the fruit of peace in the times of trial. When submission is needed, she brings forth the fruit of meekness, and self-control when yes or no is needed.

12. She has a quiet consistency and determination in her life that allows her to rejoice in the Lord no matter what's happening around her.

13. Personal answers. (Barbara Johnson, who wrote *Where Does a Mother Go to Resign?* and many other books, is not really a spiritual role model to me, but she is a lady who has taught me much about how to rejoice in the Lord when you have nothing else to rejoice in.)

14. Spiritual prosperity. We have everything we need for life and godliness. The happy Christian has an inward and outward beauty and vitality about her life that radiates the joy of the Lord. Every experience in her life will enrich her to become more prosperous for God in touching other peoples' lives.

15. Instability; drifting without direction; being tossed to and fro.

16. There is no source of peace or stability in their lives. Nothing or no one in the world can give them peace or anything to hang on to when the winds of adversity blow and the storms of life toss them about.

17. They will start talking about all the money they gave to the poor; they were baptized; and they tried to keep the Ten Commandments. The list of human works could go on and on.

18. The righteous: eternal life; the ungodly: everlasting punishment.

19. (Ask a few ladies to give brief testimonies.)

20. (Ask the ladies to take time to examine their hearts before God.)

LESSON 2

1. There is a perfect order in God's creation. He is the same yesterday, today, and forever.

2. (a) Light, darkness; (b) spring, summer, fall, winter; (c) life, death.

3. There would be total darkness. Plants would not grow. Eventually earth would be a dead planet.

4. The sun rises quickly as a bridegroom who excitedly leaves for his wedding; it makes the same circuit over and over as a man running around a track.

5. They gather to watch the sun rise or set. Why? Mankind will never

get over the splendor and the beauty of a sunrise and a sunset. No two are alike; each one is like a fresh painting on a canvas created by the artist.

6. (Ask some ladies to share their experiences with the rest of the group. I once discipled a lady who had never read or heard the Word of God before. She made this statement, "I like the God of the New Testament but not the one in the Old Testament. There is too much killing and violence in the Old Testament.")

7. The law of the LORD; the testimony of the LORD; the statues of the LORD; the commandment of the LORD; the judgments of the LORD.

8. (a) Convert the soul. No one can come to Christ without the "law of the LORD," the Word of God. (See Romans 10:17.) (b) (Ask a few ladies to share the verses God used to bring them to salvation.)

9. God's instructions for living, found in His Word, are simple to understand; even uneducated people can obey them and become wise. The simple person lives by the basics and God makes her wise. Women who try to live without God's instructions may be very intelligent in the eyes of the world, but they are considered foolish in God's sight.

10. (a) Most people find their delight in worldly things rather than in the Word of God. (b) (Have a lady share a time when she did what was right, when no one but God knew the difference, and how it brought joy to her heart.)

11. God's Word reveals to us what we should and should not do. God's Word can direct us where to go and what to do as we are going.

12. "The fear of the LORD" is a phrase of piety, meaning reverential trust, or awe, with a hatred for evil.

13. Our reverential respect for our Heavenly Lord compels us to obey Him.

14. Sometimes our judgments are colored with prejudice, resentment, jealousy, or dishonesty.

15. We have riches money cannot buy when we live by God's Word. We have love, joy, peace, contentment, happiness. Even millionaires can't buy these riches. (Note about honey: Honey is the only form of sugar food that does not need to be refined. It is perfect just as it is. In ancient times, a jar of honey on the table was a sign of wealth. Having a Bible on your table is a sign of wealth also, but only if you use it. If honey is not used, it is useless. If our Bibles are not used, they are useless.)

16. They do not heed God's Word because they do not read God's Word with a heart to learn and obey. And some people do not even read the Word on a consistent basis.

17. Verse 9—it helps us live a clean life; v. 11—it keeps us from sin; v. 45—it gives us liberty; v. 46—it makes us unashamed to talk about it; v. 52—it comforts us; v. 67—it keeps us from going astray; v. 93—it gives us life; v. 98—it makes us wise and understanding; v. 105—it gives guidance for our pathway; v. 111—it causes us to rejoice; v. 114—it provides hope; v. 128—it causes us to hate evil; v. 130—it gives light and understanding; v. 163—it causes us to hate lying; v. 165—it gives peace.

18. Verse 7—converts the soul and makes one wise; verse 8—brings rejoicing and enlightens us; verse 9—gives a standard for right and wrong; verse 10—enriches us and satisfies us; verse 11—warns us and rewards us.

19. Personal answers.

20. (a) You know what God says, but you disobey because of fear, lust, passion, greed, pride, or selfishness; deliberate, premeditated sin; double standard (won't let kids do it, but you do); willful disobedience (I know what God says, but I don't care). (b) As we meditate on God's Word in our hearts and think on His Word in our minds, the Spirit of God guides us in the right way.

21. We should be more concerned about being acceptable in God's sight than in man's. Man sees only the exterior; God knows us from the inside out (Ps. 139:1–6).

LESSON 3

1. God in Christ; the Jehovah of the Old Testament; God of power; the One Who is able to do all things and with Whom nothing is impossible, manifesting Himself in Jesus Christ.

2. Isaiah 40:25, 26—He controls the universe; Psalm 147:3–9—He takes cares of His children and His creation; Acts 17:24–28—in Him we move and have our being; He does not create and then walk away from us; He cares for us daily.

3. (Ask a few ladies to share their answers.)

4. The Good Shepherd.

5. To care for the sheep.

6. *Left:* (a) So he would know it was his sheep. (b) Sheep could not stay healthy and grow without proper nourishment. (c) He knew the sheep would stray away and could be eaten by wolves. (d) Sheep are defenseless. (e) They would die if left alone. *Right:* (a) God knows who belongs to Him. (b) He provides spiritual food, His Word, for our spiritual growth. (c) No matter where we go, He goes with us; His hands are extended to lead us and hold us up. (d) The Lord is everything we will ever need for every situation we will ever face. (e) He will carry us.

7. We can lie down in peace and sleep.

8. Still waters picture peace and tranquility. In this calm setting we can be still in God's presence and enjoy the living water.

9. (a) We must confess worry, bitterness, etc., as sin in order to have our joy restored. (b) (Allow a time for self-examination.)

10. Our reputation as Christians is at stake; but even greater than that, our Shepherd's reputation is at stake. Our walk before others demonstrates to them how great our God is.

11. Only if necessary for our spiritual survival and restoration.

12. (a) We will never be alone; the Lord will be with us. He never forsakes us. (b) (Have a few ladies share something about their valley experiences and how they handled them.)

13. (a) (Have a few ladies share some of their experiences.) (b) God corrects us because He loves us.

14. (a) Fear, doubt, guilt, bitterness, criticism, and many other evil thoughts and desires from our enemy, the Devil, can lurk in our minds and cause us much harm and hurt. (b) Thinking positive thoughts instead of negative, hurtful ones and trusting God are the only permanent remedies for the healing of our minds.

15. We should be full of joy, an overflowing joy.

16. Ephesians 4:32—He forgives us when we fail; Philippians 4:13, 19—He gives us strength to handle anything He wants us to endure; He provides all our needs—materially, emotionally, and spiritually; Isaiah 26:3—He gives us peace.

17. Titus 3:5—He saves us because of His mercy; Lamentations 3:22, 23—He does not destroy us; He is compassionate toward us; Psalm 138:8—God keeps working on us; He does not forsake us.

18. Confidence in our eternal relationship with God is a matter of trust. We must believe what God says.

LESSON 4

1. (a) David might have said, "I'm tired of fighting battles; let the young men go." (b) We might say, "I've worked in the nursery and Vacation Bible School all these years. I'm tired of serving. Let the young ladies do it."

2. No. God intends for us to stay in the race until it is over. Our bodies may fail us, and we may be forced to stay at home; but we should still be involved in spiritual matters and battles. We can always be prayer warriors—even from a bed.

3. He felt old and worn out. He felt God's chastening hand on him. He was absolutely miserable.

4. When he was confronted with his sin by Nathan.

5. (a) (Have a few ladies share their experiences of trying to hide from God.) (b) Wayward children can hide what they are doing from their parents but not from God. If they truly belong to God, He will give them no rest or peace until they come to their knees in repentance. They will feel like David did.

6. Sin—missing the mark; falling short of the standard. David knew what the Law taught about purity, but he looked and lusted for Bathsheba anyway. Iniquity—moral perversity. David committed adultery. Transgression—trespassing; going into areas where one should not be. David knew he was trespassing into another man's territory when he lay with his wife. Guile—hypocrisy. David's reason for bringing Uriah home from the battle was hypocritical. David pretended it was to give Uriah a rest, but it was really to cover David's sin.

7. He felt dirty and not fit to come into God's presence.

8. (a) David didn't justify his sin. He admitted his sin was against God and that God had the right to judge him for his sin. (b) People today use excuses such as "I can't control my actions because I was raised in a dysfunctional family."

9. David was in a backslidden condition. He at one time had had a right spirit and had had a life full of joy. He lost these when he tried to cover his sin. "He that covereth his sins shall not prosper" (Prov. 28:13).

10. (If you know of someone in the class who has come back to the Lord, ask that person ahead of time to be prepared to share a brief testimony.)

11. In the Old Testament the Holy Spirit would come and go in a person's life; e.g., Saul. In the New Testament the Spirit of God takes up permanent residence in believers.

12. She loses fellowship with God, which results in a loss of joy.

13. God says He will cleanse us from *all* unrighteousness.

14. David had a broken and contrite spirit. He hated his sin and the dishonor it brought to God. However, he did not let his sin sidetrack him and cause him to quit.

15. No sin is too great for God to forgive, and no man has fallen so low he can't get up and walk again.

16. Peter said he would never deny the Lord, but he did. He even cursed openly, while denying the Lord.

17. He might have taught them that sin is seasonal (Heb. 11:25). Sin's fun is only for a season, a few months, and then you pay the rest of the year, or, as David did, for the rest of your life. He might have taught them the law of sowing and reaping (Gal. 6:7, 8). If we sow sin in our lives, we will reap the results of our sin. Everything that is sown eventually reaps a harvest.

18. Wait in faith and pray for God to soften their hearts or bring a circumstance into their lives so they will sense their need for help.

LESSON 5

1. Sleep and food.

2. (a) Satan likes to remind us of our past failures and sins. (b) We can withstand his attacks by putting on our spiritual armor each day and facing him head on.

3. Elijah had lost hope that things would ever get better; he wanted to die. David had not lost all hope; he still felt God could help him. The depressed person has given up; she has no hope that things will ever change.

4. He felt dried up spiritually. "Panteth after the water brooks" (v. 1) and "thirsteth" (v. 2) indicate his feeling of emptiness.

5. (Have a few ladies share their experience.)

6. Romans 8:28 is one of the most common, but it is not always the most appropriate, especially if someone has just experienced a great loss or tragedy. The person is not emotionally ready to hear that this is good for her. Sometimes people say, "You just need to trust God more" or, "You just need to have more faith." Hurting people already know that truth in their heads, but they are so overwhelmed by the darkness that they cannot exercise the truth they know. Sometimes we have friends like Job's friends; they insinuate that we must have some sin in our life, and they start quoting verses relating to God's chastening.

7. "My tears have been my meat day and night." He was feeding on his unfortunate circumstances instead of on physical food to regain his strength.

8. We think about the past. We continually brood on the disappointments in life and how life used to be.

9. "I pour out my soul in me." David wasn't pouring out his soul to God or others but to himself.

10. If we pull into a shell of self-pity and tell ourselves nobody cares, we will soon be in a pit instead of a shell—a pit of depression.

11. He was honest with himself and admitted he was down and discouraged. Just as an alcoholic can't be helped until he admits he has a problem, neither can a depressed person. She must admit, "I am depressed; I need help!"

12. David might have been asking, "I know you can help me, God, but why don't You?" We all occasionally question God when we are down and discouraged. When Christ was suffering on the cross alone, He knew why He was there, yet He also cried out, "My God, my God, why hast thou forsaken me?"

13. He questioned himself; he gave his soul a talking to. He asked himself why he was so down. He might have told himself, "I've been down and moaning long enough. It's time to do something different; this is getting me nowhere."

14. (a) Instead of dwelling on his circumstances, David started to think about God and all the good things He had done for him in the past. (b) (Have a few ladies share their thoughts on how they discipline themselves to think positively.)

15. David knew God was in control of his life; nothing could touch him without God's permission or knowledge.

16. (a) David must have sung songs of praise to God in the night (compare verses 5 and 8). (b) We could listen to good Christian music on the radio or a tape to help us fall asleep. During a time when I was passing through some difficult days and nights, I left the radio on all night; if I woke up, I heard comforting music.

17. His enemies kept causing turmoil in his life. David was trying to trust God, but it seemed God wasn't answering. Didn't God care? If He did, when was He going to do something?

18. David had a deep-seated trust in God and knew that ultimately God would deliver him from his enemies. God had done it in the past; He would do it again.

19. (Have the ladies share verses they hang on to in turbulent times.)

LESSON 6

1. (a) A place of protection; a place to hide from danger. (b) When we are in trouble. We will never understand how safe our refuge is until all others have failed. Husbands and friends can do only so much for us; God can do the impossible!

2. His Word.

3. Trust Him. When we do this, we will have an untroubled heart.

4. God is greater than any problem; nothing is impossible with God!

5. (a) (Have a few ladies share their experiences.) (b) We need tight places to stretch our faith. Muscles not used grow weak; faith not stretched also grows weak.

6. We can keep our minds on the greatness of God instead of the greatness of the circumstances surrounding us. I've learned that peace of mind and presence of mind are the best way to feel secure in God's presence.

7. (Have a few ladies share, or ask one lady ahead of time whom you know has recently had an earth-shattering experience.)

8. The same God Who intervened for the Children of Israel at the Red Sea can make a way for us when there seems to be no way. But it is not enough to believe this truth in our heads; we must believe it in our hearts. We often act like the Children of Israel. Three days after God had

miraculously rescued them, they were doubting God could help them
(Exod. 15:22–24). One lady said, "Whenever trouble hits, I can't wait to
see what the Lord is going to do with this."

9. We can either run to our Refuge for help or run away from Him.
There is none to turn to but God. He is our refuge, strength, and help. If
we run from Him, we are filled with panic and hopelessness.

10. Jerusalem.

11. He promises to give us His peace. His is an unexplainable peace in
the midst of turbulent times.

12. The Holy Spirit wants to flow through us into other people's lives.
We can become a reservoir of knowledge, insight, wisdom, peace, love,
and power as the river of the Holy Spirit flows through us. Others will be
amazed at the peace we can have in difficult days as we display God's
peace before them.

13. (Have one of the ladies share an experience.)

14. Early in the morning.

15. God repeated the promises He had made to Abraham. God would give
Jacob the land, Jacob would have many descendants, and through him
all the families of the earth would be blessed. God would be with Jacob.

16. Jesus, Who has brought blessing to all the nations, came through
the seed of Jacob.

17. God has promised never to leave us, and He has never broken a
promise to His children.

18. We often quickly forget the greatness of our God and what He has
done for us in the past. Instead of asking God for wisdom, we try to figure
out how we can fix the situation. We call everyone we know to tell them
about it so they can give us some advice. Seldom do we spend time in
God's presence, reflecting on His power and promises, before we do
anything else.

19. In the Old Testament the verb "to know" was often used to describe
the sexual relationship between a man and a woman. The Lord wants our
relationship to go beyond knowing Him as Savior. He wants our relationship with Him to be a close, intimate relationship. He wants us to know
Him better and better each day.

20. (Have a few ladies share how they spend their devotional times
with the Lord.)

21. It is hard to trust a person if you don't know the person real well.
When we really learn to trust God, we know He will be our refuge, our
strength, and our help. He will help us not to fear or faint because we
know He will fight for us. He works when nothing else does.

LESSON 7

1. God is good.

2. He had almost lost faith in God's goodness. He had almost decided
wickedness paid.

3. (Personal answers. One example is a godly person who struggles for
years to get on his/her feet financially, then, through tragic circumstances,
loses everything. This person could easily slip into bitterness and resentment if he/she forgets that God is good even when He doesn't seem good.)

4. (a) Foolish, boastful wicked people. (b) Compared to a godly person's struggles, the wicked seem to have it made.

5. He seemed to think they were free from the terror of death and the troubles of life.

6. Their violent, arrogant, and irreverent spirit.

7. (a) This person seems to have everything going for him/her, with everything he/she wants. (b) (Answers include money, health, home, family, influence. Have the ladies share their thoughts.)

8. They belittle God by asking, "Is your God blind and deaf? Does He know what's going on down here? Is your God dumb and helpless? Why doesn't He help you?"

9. He couldn't see that living for God had gained him anything, yet the wicked seemed to have everything good going for them.

10. He realized he could cause other believers to stumble if he voiced his doubts. He could talk only to God about all the frustration in his mind. He felt he was at his wit's end. He was driving himself crazy thinking about it.

11. (Have some of the ladies share their thoughts. I've always been helped when I get my eyes off my circumstances and back on the Lord. I do this by meditating on Scripture. Sometimes we also need to talk to someone who can encourage us.)

12. He began to see things in their right perspective. He had forgotten this life is so short compared to eternal life. He might have said, "How could I have been so blind?"

13. Eternal destruction. When death comes, the wicked are in a "slippery place." They have nothing to hang on to. Death will come in a moment, but destruction is eternal.

14. He regretted that he had ever doubted God's goodness or the way God manages the lives of the wicked and the godly.

15. (Have a few ladies share their experiences.)

16. When we fall and disappoint ourselves and God, we won't stay down if we get our eyes back on the Lord. He will lift us up again. God never leaves us or forsakes us (Heb. 13:5).

17. The Lord will guide our steps here on earth and let us walk on streets of gold in Glory.

18. God was going to be his supreme delight on earth and certainly would be in Heaven. No longer would he be grasping for what he could get, but he would dwell on how rich he was—Asaph knew God!

19. The wicked will perish. Their end is destruction.

20. This experience has been good for me. It has drawn me closer to God and taught me to trust God more than I ever did before.

21. (Have a few ladies share their experiences.)

LESSON 8

1. "He that dwelleth in the secret place of the most High."

2. Not too many people know about it.

3. To live in close fellowship with the Lord, abiding in His presence daily. Just as the branch draws its strength from the vine, we draw our spiritual strength from Christ, the vine.

4. (a) We must spend time with a person to really get to know him/her. (b) By spending time in the Word and in God's presence, we get to know Him.

5. Safe under the shadow of the Almighty (vv. 1, 2); delivered from Satan's traps and desires (v. 3); covered with the Almighty's wings and feathers (v. 4); protected with His shield and armor (v. 4); no fear, day or night (vv. 5, 6); protection in the midst of great danger (v. 7); no evil or plague (v. 10); kept (protected) by angels (v. 11); deliverance (v. 14); set on high (v. 14); God's answer when we call (v. 15); protection and deliverance in trouble (v. 15); honor (v. 15); full, satisfying life (v. 16); God's salvation, or deliverance (v. 16).

6. We must stay close to a person for his shadow to fall on us.

7. (a) A refuge is a quiet and secure hiding place. A fortress is a place of defense against the enemy. God is both of these for us. (b) God was everything the psalmist would ever need.

8. Satan tries to snare us when we don't walk close to Christ.

9. God speaks of His feathers and His wings and compares Himself to a mother hen who protects her little ones. These little chicks must stay close to enjoy the mother's protection. The same relates to us; we need to stay close to the Father.

10. A shield and buckler, or coat of armor. We are fully covered.

11. Our lives are in God's hands. Nothing can touch us without God's permission. Satan may wound us, but he cannot destroy us. God is always by our side and can see in the dark; darkness and light are the same to Him.

12. He had made God his "habitation," his hiding place.

13. (Ask the ladies to share their experiences.)

14. We do not have to fear Satan, but we must be prepared for his attacks. When we put on the armor of God, including the covering for our feet, lions and adders can easily be crushed beneath our feet.

15. He expects the same steadfast affection from us. We are to love Him with all our heart, strength, and mind.

16. He sets them on high. Could this mean they live above their circumstances because their intimate knowledge of God allows them to trust Him?

17. Yes, no, or wait.

18. (Have a few ladies share brief testimonies.)

LESSON 9

1. Seek the Lord by spending time in the Word and prayer.

2. (Have the ladies share some ideas.)

3. When God showers us with unexpected blessings or spares our life from a close call with death or delivers us from some other catastrophe.

4. When we lose a loved one, our job is terminated, we get a cancer diagnosis, or a child is wayward. (You might want to give the ladies inexpensive prints of the quotation that follows question 4. See the ordering information in the notes on page 88.)

5. If we believe God is good only when the circumstances in our lives are good, we can never have the joy and gladness God wants us to have

(John 15:11). This is a joy that remains. It is a result of abiding in Christ, drawing our strength from Him daily (John 15:4, 5).

6. We often get tired of showing mercy. We feel people should get the consequences they deserve for their unjust deeds. God never runs out of mercy. This is another reason we should serve Him with gladness.

7. Marriage vows are broken. Financial commitments are made but never paid. A job promotion is promised but never materializes.

8. Major on speaking words of praise and adoration to God and uplifting words to others.

9. We do it for God's glory so others can see the joy of the Lord in our lives and be refreshed.

10. If we get our rewards down here, we won't get them in Heaven. We will also feel unappreciated and misused if we are serving only for praise from men.

11. Our service should be for the Lord, not for the praise of men. When we focus on God's continual and unconditional love for us and His continual forgiveness toward us, it will change how we view those we serve.

12. God is in control of all creation and of each person He created. He does as He pleases, when and where He pleases, without asking our permission.

13. (Some ladies may be willing to share their answers.)

14. Our focus must be on character—becoming more like Christ—instead of on comfort and ease in life.

15. Since we are His people, He has the right to tell us what we should do. And because we are sheep, we need a shepherd to guide our lives.

16. (a) Sheep are prone to wander away from the fold and get themselves into hurtful or dangerous places. (b) Christians are also prone to wander away from their Shepherd when they forget His sovereign control in their lives.

17. (Have a few ladies share.)

18. Personal answers.

LESSON 10

1. The Israelites had forgotten their God, but He had not forgotten them. Their sin did not exhaust God's mercy and kindness toward His children.

2. (We could never list all God's mighty acts in our lives because He daily loadeth us with benefits [Ps. 68:19]. Ask the ladies to share a few things on their lists.)

3. Those who "keep judgment," or who are fair in their dealings with others, and those who do what is right.

4. God is merciful to us as well. When we sin, He forgives us and gives us another opportunity to live for Him just as He did for the Children of Israel.

5. Thy chosen; thy nation; thine inheritance.

6. We have sinned; we have committed iniquity; we have done wickedly.

7. Sin—missing the mark; to stumble or fall. We sin because we are born with a nature to sin. We practice sin because we choose to sin rather than obey God. Iniquity—that which is crooked, bent, perverse. Wickedness—lowliness, restlessness.

8. (1) God turned all the streams, rivers, ponds, and pools of water into blood. (2) God covered the land of Egypt with frogs. (3) God turned all the dust of the land into lice to cover men and beast. (4) God sent flies into the homes and land of Egypt. (5) God killed all the Egyptians' cattle but spared the Israelites' cattle. (6) God turned ashes into dust that fell on men and cattle and covered them with boils. (7) God sent fire and hail that covered the land of Egypt but not the land of Goshen where the Israelites lived. (8) God covered the land with locusts. (9) God sent total darkness over Egypt for three days. (10) God killed the firstborn in the households of all the Egyptians, but none of the Children of Israel who had put the blood of a lamb on their doorposts was touched.

9. His mercy and favor on them. The firstborn in each Egyptian house died, but God spared the children of obedient Israelites.

10. They were hardly out of Egypt, where God had performed one miracle after another, when they began to doubt God's power to deliver them. They questioned His faithfulness to them. They wanted to return to Egyptian bondage.

11. He overlooked their lack of faith, and He extended mercy. He saved them from the Egyptians by opening the Red Sea so they could walk through on dry land.

12. The Egyptians pursued the Israelites into the sea, but after the Israelites were safe on dry ground, God closed the walls of water and drowned the entire Egyptian army.

13. They believed God again and sang praises to Him.

14. As soon as a crisis arises, we forget God's faithfulness to us in the past. Often we are filled with fear instead of faith. Our fear makes us forget to look for God's hand at work in our circumstances. Most of us can sing and praise God when God gets us through the trial, but few of us sing and see God in the midst of the fire.

15. They were murmuring again; they wanted water.

16. Six weeks; they were hungry.

17. (a) Flesh (meat) to eat. (b) No. In fact, it was a curse on them.

18. The prodigal son is a good picture of someone who got what he wanted, but it brought leanness to his soul. A person lusting for more and more things can easily be drawn away from God. She doesn't need to trust God now that she has what she wanted.

19. (a) God judged Korah, Dathan, and Abiram by opening up the earth and swallowing up the three men and their families and everything they owned. (b) They were burned up.

20. We should respect God's chosen leaders.

LESSON 11

1. From the idol worship they had seen in Egypt.

2. They were giving credit to the golden calf instead of God for bringing them out of Egypt. God surely knew the hearts of these people when He gave the first two commandments.

3. The things of this world are a constant temptation to us.

4. (Have one or two volunteers share their experiences.)

5. God would have completely destroyed them. He would have started

a new nation with Moses. They would have been the people of Moses instead of the people of Abraham.

6. They didn't want to enter the land; they were fearful. They didn't believe God would take care of them. They were ready to go back to Egypt.

7. No one over age twenty entered the Promised Land; they all died in the wilderness.

8. Of the twelve spies, only Joshua and Caleb believed God and wanted to enter the land.

9. We are often fearful and forget that God orders our steps. He will guide us and go before us to prepare the way.

10. The Israelites joined the Moabites in the worship of Baal-peor. These sinful, cultic practices included necromancy (communication with the dead).

11. (a) 24,000. (b) Phinehas (Aaron's grandson).

12. Moses dishonored God by disobeying Him. God told him to speak to the rock and then water would come forth. In anger, Moses struck the rock twice. He forfeited his privilege of leading the Children of Israel into the Promised Land.

13. Our constant complaining can wear them down. They may never accomplish what God called them to do.

14. The Canaanite nations were heathen idol worshipers. They would draw the Israelites away from God.

15. Wickedness is infectious.

16. He abhorred, or detested, it.

17. God allowed the Israelites' enemies to oppress them and bring them into subjection.

18. Even while God was disciplining His children, He remembered them in pity. He delivered them over and over again.

19. So God's name would be exalted in the nation again.

20. Some people are professors but not possessors. They profess to know Christ as Savior, but they do not truly possess eternal life. God will chasten those who truly belong to Him to restore them to fellowship (Heb. 12:6–11).

LESSON 12

1. Omniscient—knowing all things. Omnipresent—present in all places at all times. Omnipotent—having unlimited power or authority. Righteous—always doing what is right.

2. God knows me better than anyone else—better than my parents or mate. He knows me inside out. This thought leaves me completely naked before God. He pries into the most secret corners of my life. He knows the thoughts I have never shared with anyone else. He even knows the number of hairs on my head (Matt. 10:30).

3. God knows why we do what we do because He is the only one Who knows "the thoughts and intents of the heart." He knows our hidden motives and secret fantasies.

4. When we are transparent, we take off our masks and let down our guard. We need to let people know what we are really thinking and feeling so they can help and encourage us.

5. Nothing can touch us that God does not allow, or permit.

6. It would fill us with awe because not one sin can be hidden from God and courage because God is that intimately involved in our lives.

7. Leads her and holds her.

8. Because she wants to live in sin and foolishly thinks that if she turns her back on God, He will leave her alone.

9. Possessed—created or formed. Reins—inward parts. In the Hebrew this word literally means "kidneys." The Hebrews used "kidneys" for the center of a person's emotions and conscience. Covered—weaved.

10. Here is my paraphrase: "Lord, You formed my inward parts, my emotions, my conscience. You did all this while I was in my mother's womb. You weaved every part of me together—my arms to my shoulders, my legs to my hips, and my head to my shoulders."

11. One example: My eyes have 107 million cells in them, and 7 million are cones. These cones help me distinguish a thousand shades of color. (Ask several ladies to share their examples.)

12. We are each one-of-a-kind, unique creations of God. He fashions each of us according to His plan and design.

13. Counting the sand of the sea would take forever. God's thoughts toward us will go on forever. We will never be out of His mind or heart.

14. Thoughts of peace, not evil, and a future full of hope.

15. When he thought about God's love, care, and concern for him, it angered him to hear the wicked speak against God and take His name in vain.

16. David's hatred for his enemies resulted from his zeal for God. God's enemy was his enemy. He desired God's righteous justice, not his own personal vengeance.

17. David asked God to search his mind and heart to see if there were any wrong motives behind his strong words against his enemies.

18. When we are struggling with feelings of revenge and anger and have confessed them as sin. We want to be sure we have every ounce of the poison out of us. David asked God to do what verse 1 said God had done, "Thou hast searched me, and known me."

19. The Word of God can do an exploratory surgery on us each time we read it and then heed it. It will point out our selfishness, worldliness, disobedience, pride, and unbelief. However, we can choose to leave the sin in our lives and let it destroy us, or we can painfully deal with it and remove it.